BY AVON RIVER

THE MACMILLAN COMPANY
NEW YORK • BOSTON • CHICAGO
DALLAS • ATLANTA • SAN FRANCISCO

MACMILLAN AND CO., LIMITED
LONDON • BOMBAY • CALCUTTA
MADRAS • MELBOURNE

THE MACMILLAN COMPANY
OF CANADA, LIMITED
TORONTO

BY AVON RIVER

✣ ✣ ✣

H. D.

THE MACMILLAN COMPANY

New York · 1949

First Printing

PRINTED IN THE UNITED STATES OF AMERICA

GOOD FREND

Shakespeare Day, 23rd April, 1945

GOOD FREND FOR IESVS SAKE FORBEARE,
TO DIGG THE DVST ENCLOASED HEARE!
BLESTE BE Y^E^ MAN Y^T^ SPARES THES STONES,
AND CVRST BE HE Y^T^ MOVES MY BONES.

23rd April, 1564
23rd April, 1616

For

BRYHER

Shakespeare Day
April 23, 1945

&

ROBERT HERRING

St. George Day
April 23, 1945

✣ ✣ ✣ PART I ✣ ✣ ✣

The Tempest

I

Come as you will, but I came home
Driven by *The Tempest;* you may come,

With banner or the beat of drum;
You may come with laughing friends,

Or tired, alone; you may come
In triumph, many kings have come

And queens and ladies with their lords,
To lay their lilies in this place,

Where others, known for wit and song,
Have left their laurel; you may come,

Remembering how your young love wept
With Montague long ago and Capulet.

II

I came home driven by *The Tempest;*
That was after the wedding-feast;
'Twas a sweet marriage, we are told;
And she *a paragon . . . who is now queen,*
And the rarest that e'er came there;

We know little of *the king's fair daughter*
Claribel; her father was Alonso,
King of Naples, her brother, Ferdinand,

And we read later, *in one voyage*
Did Claribel her husband find at Tunis:

Claribel was outside all of this,
The Tempest came after they left her;
Read for yourself, *Dramatis Personae.*

III

Read for yourself, *Dramatis Personae,*
Alonso, Sebastian, Prospero,
Antonio, Ferdinand, Gonzalo,
Adrian, Francisco, Caliban
(Whom some call Pan),
Trinculo, Stephano, Miranda,
Ariel, Iris, Ceres, Juno;

These are the players, chiefly,
Caliban, a savage and deformed slave,
Ariel, an airy Spirit, Miranda,
The magician's lovely daughter,
The magician—ah indeed, I had forgot
Boatswain, Mariners, Nymphs and Reapers,

And among these, are other
Spirits attending on Prospero.

IV

Read through again, *Dramatis Personae;*
She is not there at all, but Claribel,
Claribel, the birds shrill, Claribel,
Claribel echoes from this rainbow-shell,
I stooped just now to gather from the sand;

Where? From an island somewhere . . .
Some say the *Sea-Adventure* set out,
(In May, 1609, to be exact)
For the new colony, Virginia;

Some say the *Sea-Adventure* ran aground
On the Bermudas; but all on board
Were saved, built new ships
And sailed on, a year later;

It is all written in an old pamphlet,
Did he read of her there, Claribel?

V

The flagship, the *Sea-Adventure*
Was one of nine ships; it bore
Sir Thomas Gates and Sir George Somers;
So the poet read, some say
Of the five hundred colonists;
(O the wind, the spray,
The birds wheeling out of the mist,
The strange birds, whistling from strange trees,
Bermuda); there was more than one pamphlet,
(The newspaper of his day),
He searched them all;
Gates, Somers—who were they?

Englishmen like himself, who felt the lure
Of the sea-ways—here we are in London—
A new court festival, a masque?
Elizabeth, our princess, is to wed
The Elector Palatine—who's that?
Frederick, I think. And where's the place—
Bohemia? I don't think so,
But anyhow it doesn't matter,
A foreign fellow is to wed our princess,
The grand-daughter of Scotland's Mary;
Occasion—compliment—another play!

VI

That was yesterday or day before yesterday;
To-day (April 23, 1945, to be exact),

We stand together; it always rains
On Shakespeare's Day, the townsfolk say,
But to-day, there is soft mist only . . .

Slowly, there are so many of us,
We pass through the churchyard gate,
And pausing wait and read old names
On the stones under our feet;
Look—there's a Lucy—O, the hunter's heart,
The hunter's stealth,
But listen to this,
He's caught at last—who?
John Shakespeare's lad—up to no good—
Sir Thomas Lucy caught him at it—
Poaching—(O feet of wind,
O soul of fire, so Lucy caught you
Stalking deer?)—poaching?

VII

He stole everything,
There isn't an original plot
In the whole lot of his plays;
They're scattered everywhere, hotchpotch;
A little success with the old Queen?

Well, yes—by patching up
Other men's plots and filling in
With odds and ends he called his own,
But now—he's gone back home,

And time he went;
He couldn't compete with the new wits,
New fashions—that last, he called *The Tempest,*
Was taken out of the news-sheet,
Stale news at that and best forgot,

The *Sea-Adventure* and that lot,
Gates, Somers—who are they anyway?

Or who *were* they? They'll come to no good,
(No one ever did) in that colony,
What d'you call it? Virginia?
Look at Drake, Raleigh.

VIII

Awkwardly, tenderly,
We stand with our flowers,
Separate, self-consciously,
Shyly or in child-like
Delicate simplicity;

Each one waits patiently,
Now we are near the door;
Till sudden, wondrously,
All shyness drops away,
Awkwardness, complacency;

Ring, ring and ring again,
'Twas a sweet marriage,
So they say, *my beloved is mine*
And I am his; Claribel
The chimes peel;

Claribel, the chimes say,
The king's fair daughter
Marries Tunis; O spikenard,
Myrrh and myrtle-spray,
'Twas a sweet marriage;

Tenderly, tenderly,
We stand with our flowers,
Our belovèd is ours,
Our belovèd is ours,
To-day? Yesterday?

PART II

Rosemary

BLEST BE Y^{E} MAN Y^{T} SPARES THES STONES.

I

My fingers knew each syllable,
I sensed the music in the stone,
I knew a rhythm would pass on,
And out of it, if I could stoop
And run my bare palm over it
And touch the letters and the words,
Reading the whole as the blind read.

My fingers knew each syllable,
As a lute-player with a lute,
Whose hand lies waiting on the frame,
Who knows the wires are taut and bright,
Who waits a gesture from a throne,
Or from a balcony, or down,
Among the crowd, from his own lady.

If I could touch the stone, I knew
That virtue would go out of it;
I plotted to efface myself,
To steal un-noticed to the rail,
To kneel and touch if but one letter;
I wondered if the script were worn
And dim and old, or if it shone,
With light and shadow on the stone.

But when I stood before the altar,
The stone had vanished as if under

Azure and green of deep-sea water,
Hyacinth-green and hyacinth-blue;
So once a discus idly thrown,
Had slain the Spring and yet forever,
That death had blossomed, for the power
Of Love transformed Death to a flower.

There were no letters anywhere,
But on each bud, each leaf, each spray,
The words were written that beneath
The laurel, iris, rosemary,
Heartsease and every sort of lily,
Speak through all flowers eternally,

Blest be ye man—that one who knows
His heart glows in the growing rose.

II

And still the bells sway,
My belovèd is mine
and I am his;
And still the bells say,

The king's fair daughter
Marries Tunis; O spikenard,
Myrrh and myrtle-spray,
'Twas a sweet marriage.

III

Say Claribel,
Say asphodel,
No flower of death,
But fragrant breath
Of life;

See everywhere,
Bright flower-de-luce,

Sword-flower and king-spear
For a truce;
                For strife

Is ended,
We ascended
From gloom and fear,
Not after death
                But now and here.

IV

Who hold him dear,
Bring woody stem
With leaf and flower,
The sweet herb,
                Rosemary,

Known from old time,
In sacred office,
To trim the bride,
To deck the shroud,
                Ros maris,

Dew of the sea,
Salt with sea-spray,
So was his music
Drawn from wood,
                Rosemary.

V

But not lute alone
Nor lyre-frame,
Carpenter square and tool
Were made from the tree,
                Rosemary;

Many, many the bees
Hummed in that tree,

Much sweet was plundered,
Stacked and stored,
Rosemary;

O, what a house he built
To shelter all of us,
O what a plesaunce,
Planed by his rule,
Rosemary.

VI

Time has an end, they say,
Sea-walls are worn away
By wind and the sea-spray,
Not the herb,
Rosemary.

Queens have died, I am told,
Faded the cloth-of-gold,
No Caesar half so bold,
As the herb,
Rosemary.

Rooted within the grave,
Spreading to heaven, save
Us by the grace he gave
To the herb,
Rosemary.

VII

What rose of memory,
Ros maris,
From what sea of bliss!

VIII

Full fathom five
and under

The sea-surge
thunder,
Rosalind and Rosaline
With Juliet and Julia
Join hands with Maria,
Mariana and Marina,
Katherine and Katherina
And with many other bright
Spirits;
Iras,
Iris,
Isabel,
Helen, Helena; Helenus
With other princes leads the host
From Arden, Navarre and Illyria,
Venice, Verona and Sicilia;

Knowing these and others well,
Seeing these whom I have loved,
Hearing these—why did I choose
The invisible, voiceless Claribel?

IX

She never had a word to say,
An emblem, a mere marriage token,

Nor even trod a rondelay
Or watched a play within the play

With other ladies—and yet—
I wonder when the time was short,

And he had said farewell to court,
And pondered, fingering the script,

Can this then, really be the last?
If he remembered Claribel.

X

For still the bells sway,
My belovèd is mine
              and I am his,
And still the bells say,

The king's fair daughter
Marries Tunis; O spikenard,
Myrrh and myrtle-spray,
'Twas a sweet marriage.

XI

I only threw a shadow
On his page,
Yet I was his,
He spoke my name;

He hesitated,
Raised his quill,
Which paused,
Waited a moment,

And then fell
Upon the unblotted line;
I was born,
Claribel.

XII

What's in a name?
Everything, life, death,
Infamy or fame.

It is enough,
I live forever,

He called me fair
In one short line.

XIII

I had no voice
To chide the lark at dawn,
Or argue with a Jew,
Be merciful;

I had no wit
To banter with a clown,
Or claim a kingdom
Or denounce a throne;

I had no hand
To snatch a dagger,
Or pluck wild-flowers,
For a crown.

XIV

I stand invisible on the water-stair,
Nor envy Egypt,
Drifting through the lilies;
I may go here or there,
Bargain for bracelets on the bridge in Venice,
Or buy ripe cherries in Verona's market;

Call me most proud who wait,
Even upon the very outskirts of the crowd,
At carnival,
Or stand among the strangers at the gate,
Watching a burial.

XV

And then I wondered . . .
When wandering by Avon's water,

Who best attended him,
Squire and page and jester from Arden,
Dim shapes or shapes seen and sensed clearly
And laughter heard and song and history,
Unrolled further into the past,
    Unrolled mysteriously
    Into the future;

    And then I wondered . . .
    What voice it was from Avallon,
    Calling that last April,
    Farewell, farewell,
    But only to pain, regret, disaster,
    O friend, farewell
    Is only to fear, despair, torture,
    Say not farewell,
    But hail, Master.
        Was it Ariel?
        Was it Claribel?

PART III

Claribel's Way to God

I

I met a Poor Clare with a chaplet
Of beads who muttered as she went,
And ran her fingers over it,
With much of *ora* and of *ave*.

She called the thing a rosary,
And when I asked her what she meant,
She said it was for Rose-of Mary,
Heaven-dowered, heaven-sent.

I asked the Clare why she was poor,
She said she was Saint Francis' daughter,
And dedicate to poverty,
Obedience and chastity.

There was some music in the thing,
That rattled on now of *pro nobis,*
And Rose-of-Mary minded me
Of the *ros maris.*

And so I got a woodcarver,
To hew me out just some such beads,
But mine were made of rosemary,
And fashioned and strung differently.

II

I met a friar in a hood,
And asked him who Saint Francis was,

He said, a holy man and good,
He preached to wolves and even men,

He talked and whistled to the birds;
I asked the friar, where and when?
The friar said, O, that was after
He gave away his cloak and then,

His shoes; I said, but how
Could he endure the frost and snow?
The friar said it was no durance,
But joy to do his Lady penance.

I asked, who could this lady be?
The friar said, simplicity
And purity and holy love,
And her sweet name was Poverty.

And of her Lord, Sir, who is he?
The friar said, God and God's Son,
The spoken and the written Word,
These Three . . . but One.

III

I, too, was Clare but Clare-the-fair,
Claribel, not a Poor Clare,
For I was much too well endowed,
Yet ignorant, I would entreat

A learned scholar or a prelate,
To show me what I did not know,
To tell me what I dared not ask
The Poor Clare or the wandering friar.

I met a prelate at the gate,
His robe was rich with ornament,

He had a strong body-guard before,
And many servants followed after;

I followed with them to the door;
One with his halberd waited there,
He looked with awe at my attire,
Stood at attention when I spoke,

I pray your Lord a word with me;
He bowed before the Queen of Tunis
And said I'll wait before the dais
And name you to His Holiness.

IV

He must have seen nobility
Embroidered on my sleeve, for I
Was swiftly ushered through the crowd;
The prelate greeted me—my daughter?

He raised two fingers and I bowed;
I said, I come to ask of God;
He said, ah fair, ah worthy lady,
This passion for philosophy

Becomes you well, and many follow
The lure of Rhetoriç and I hear
The court is all for argument,
Plato, Plotinus, Origen.

Proclus, Ficinus—I presume
You follow Plato, shun the Stoics?
And without waiting for an answer,
The Arian heresy creeps back,

Look to Jerome and Augustine,
Ambrose and Cyprian when in doubt;

He nodded to the servitor,
He raised two fingers and I bowed.

V

I wandered much in Italy,
To find the answer; in Assisi,
I saw a picture of a poor friar,
Francis himself, the mountain wolf,

The birds in branches in a row;
I saw his sandal and a cloak,
Worn and thread-bare that was his;
I begged admission to the Clares,

And a long time, brewed rue and thyme
And stuffed rose-petals in tall jars,
And all the jars were marked with names,
Orris, marjaram, jasimine.

I told the Mother, I must leave,
For still my rosary was wrought,
Differently from the other Clares,
And strung and fashioned unlike theirs,

For other names and other prayers;
For though I learnt what *ora* meant,
And knew *pro nobis* was for us,
Their *aves* were not for my rosemary.

VI

I wandered near, I wandered far,
And met with wondrous courtesy;
They thought me one of them—only
One seemed to stare and wonder.

The others thought that I had lived,
The others thought that I had died,

They never seemed to sense or know
That I was a mere marriage token,

Who never had a word to say;
But he, it seemed, regarded me,
As if myself, I were the play,
Players and a great company.

He said, *I died, I die again,*
But this time, shrived and satisfied;
I said, wait sir; for I would know,
Where you have been, where you will go.

He said, I went to Acre and back,
But now I learn, the screw and wrack
Are torturing my brother Templars;
Was it for this—the Sepulchre?

VII

I was in Venice once again,
Where ships were docked and wounded men
Lay on their pallets, or on straw,
Thrown down before the Ducal Palace

And in Mark's square and Piazetta
And all along the crowded Riva;
Under an arch, he lay alone,
Like a crusader cut of stone;

A lantern cast its shadow on
The cross, emblazoned on his tunic,
Now it is night again, he said
Come Lady, say what you will say,

Are we condemned and damned, we brothers,
We followers of the Holy Cross?

I said, sir, this is rosemary,
I am no priest, a nursing-sister

Has little time for argument;
I never followed what they meant
By schism and by heresy,
But this will take your pain away.

VIII

I laid the spray upon his tunic,
He said, ah Mary, nay, not Mary,
But Wisdom, the Supernal Light;
The trouvères hid in the aubade,

Worship of light, the Arabs told
A tale of passion and of beauty,
Disguised as Lover and as Lady,
To hide the ineffable Mystery;

In Persia, too, and we of Acre
Worshipped the same, pledged to one God;
I said, the Clares were very good,
And gave me this robe for the robe,

I laid aside, for though I could
Not tell their rosary nor their *aves,*
They praised me much for that I knew
The lore of every plant that grew.

He said, *your robe is very white,*
Bend down; he said, *are these the eyes?*
He drew me close, I heard his voice,
But once—this side of Paradise.

IX

Consolamentum here and now,
I heard as my lips touched his brow;

To him alone, I told my secret,
Sir, I am nothing but a name,

Claribel; Brightly-fair, he said,
O clearly beautiful, thou Spirit;
So he alone among them all
Knew I was other than I seemed,

Nor nursing-sister nor a queen,
And he it was that broke the spell,
For as he said, farewell, farewell,
An echo from across the water,

Answered from bell-tower and cathedral;
The lantern flickered and went out,
And yet the buds of the *ros maris*
Shone like dew fallen on his cross.

He said, I died, I die again,
But this time shrived and satisfied,
And as the bell from San Giovanni
Answered San Marco, the dawn came.

X

Though still San Marco pealed and rang,
The pavement seemed to melt away,
Though still I heard Giovanni answer,
I found I knelt in Avon meadow,

I found I stood by Avon river,
But Ariel was there before;
And as he sang farewell, farewell,
My chaplet told its *ora, ave*

To Ariel's song, *farewell, farewell*
Is only to pain, disaster; farewell

Is only to fear, despair, torture,
Say not farewell, but hail, Master!

And then but one chime pealed so sweetly.
I thought it Mary-of-the-Lily,
But it was Avon's Trinity;
And suddenly, I saw it clear,

And suddenly, I saw it fair,
How Love is God, how Love is strong,
When One is Three and Three are One,
The Dream, the Dreamer and the Song.

THE GUEST

Go, Soul, the Body's guest,
  Upon a thankless arrant,
Fear not to touch the best;
  The truth shall be thy warrant;
    Go, since I needs must die,
    And give the World the lie!

To

BRYHER

from

Seehof
Küsnacht

My thanks are due to Norman Holmes Pearson for revision of the poems and some of the dates, quoted in The Guest. *In certain instances I have retained earlier traditional dates, since disputed or disproved, and I have also endeavoured to preserve the living tradition, though sometimes at variance with the discoveries of modern scholarship.*

❖ ❖ ❖ ❖ ❖ ❖

REMEMBERING SHAKESPEARE always, but remembering him differently. Reach from your bed in dark night, half in a dream or delirium. What do you seek? Your hand, touching the bed-table, remembers the telephone—but that was in your own room in London. You are somewhere else; you want something? There are no friends near. You murmur a number, 1–5–6–4 and follow it with another, 1–6–1–6. But that is no telephone number.

1–5–6–4. This is the year that Christopher Marlowe was born in Canterbury. This is the year that William Shakespeare was born at Stratford-on-Avon. With a slight alteration, a mere matter of ten years, we have 1–5–5–4. Philip Sidney was born exactly ten years before Shakespeare and Marlowe. Some say this Christopher became an actor, after leaving Oxford, some that he went with Sidney to the wars. Small wars but wars in the Low Countries and with The Huguenots in France. Sir Philip Sidney witnessed the Massacre of Saint Bartholomew. Later "when Queen Elizabeth sent English troops to help the Dutch in their struggle for freedom," he "fell fighting at Zutphen, in September, 1586."

"He remains the most conspicuous figure of chivalry among English personalities."

Let us step back that ten years.

Fulke Greville, Lord Brooke of Beauchamp Court, Warwickshire, lived for those days to the considerable age of seventy-four. His friend, Sir Philip Sidney, was thirty-two, that September. They were both thirty-two, that September. But after forty-two years of separation, the honourable member of the Privy Council had one last word to say. He would have engraved on his tombstone, this: "The Friend of Sir Philip Sidney."

Now another step backward, not far, 1553. This is the date of the birth of Edmund Spenser, in London.

It was due to the influence of Sir Philip Sidney that Spenser received advancement as secretary to the Lord Lieutenant of Ireland, and a grant from the Crown. His castle and manor were later burnt and plundered. Edmund Spenser came home with his wife and children, where it is said he died, "in extreme indigence and want of bread."

Subtract one more number. 1552 is the date of the birth of Sir Walter Raleigh. He was born in Devonshire. "He served five years in France with the Huguenots" and later in the Netherlands. In 1579, he with his half-brother, Sir Humphrey Gilbert, planned their first trip to America. He was beheaded October, 1618.

We have come back to Stratford. It is just two years since William Shakespeare died at New Place, April 23, 1616.

Christopher Marlowe, born in the same year, died at the age of twenty-nine, stabbed in that mysterious tavern brawl, outside London.

We have, in the more complete anthologies of *Songs and Lyrics* from the Elizabethan poets and dramatists, more than one hundred names. Not one is negligible. I have mentioned eight of these, seven men and one woman. Queen Elizabeth is commonly the only woman listed among the more than one hundred Elizabethan lyrists.

> Blow, blow thou winter wind,
> Thou art not so unkind

As man's ingratitude;
Thy tooth is not so keen,
Because thou art not seen,
Although thy breath be rude.

Freeze, freeze thou bitter sky,
That dost not bite so nigh
As benefits forgot:
Though thou the waters warp,
Thy sting is not so sharp
As friend remembered not.

We have imagined only one true way of recalling these, our poets. A cursory glance at Sidney's *Arcadia,* a more careful reading of Spenser's *Faerie Queene,* a re-reading of Fletcher's *Faithful Shepherdess* and an intensified study of *Tragedies, Comedies* and *Historical Plays* of William Shakespeare, will not do it. Let us begin with Sir Edward Dyer, 1540. He was a friend of Doctor John Dee, adviser and astrologer of the Queen. Sir Edward rose to fame as treasurer of the realm in the heyday of Elizabethan grandeur. He came to grief, as he forsook Doctor John Dee and his confederates at Prague, explaining bluntly to the Queen that her hopes of future alchemical treasure were founded on a fraud. He was no mean poet.

He died in 1607, in poverty.

My mind to me a kingdom is;
Such present joys therein I find,
That it excels all other bliss
That earth affords or grows by kind:
Though much I want which most would have,
Yet still my mind forbids to crave.

Edmund Spenser returned home to die; Sidney met his death through reckless chivalry; Marlowe, an even more romantic end, in that mysterious tavern brawl; Raleigh, the legendary figure of romance, was beheaded in the Tower; Sir Edward Dyer, like Edmund Spenser, died in poverty and disgrace; and though "The Friend of Sir Philip Sidney" lived, for Elizabethan times, to the astonishing age of seventy-four, Fulke Greville, Lord Brooke is said at the end to have been stabbed by one of his own servants. We have named seven of these. Of William Shakespeare, alone, can we visualize a chair drawn up before an open window, an apple-tree in blossom, a friend or two and children. There was Elizabeth and, with her, Judith. Hamnet, Judith's twin, is not forgotten.

We do not know what he is thinking. Queen Elizabeth has been dead now, thirteen years. Sir Walter Raleigh is still alive, he has two years yet to live, eating his heart out in the Tower. An accomplished courtier is, of necessity, a poet.

Go, Soul, the Body's guest,
  Upon a thankless arrant,
Fear not to touch the best;
  The truth shall be thy warrant;
    Go, since I needs must die,
    And give the World the lie!

Say to the Court, it glows
  And shines like rotten wood;
Say to the Church, it shows
  What's good and doth no good;
    If Church and Court reply,
    Then give them both the lie.

We wander through a labyrinth. If we cut straight through, we destroy the shell-like curves and involutions. Where logic is, where reason dictates, we have walls, broad highways, bridges, causeways. But we are in a garden.

Philomel, with melody
Sing in our sweet lullaby;

Lulla, lulla, lullaby, lulla, lulla, lullaby;
Never harm,
Nor spell nor charm,
Come our lovely lady nigh;
So, good night with lullaby.

And ladysmocks all silver white
Do paint the meadows with delight.

Ladysmocks? They lie pale lavender across the unmown strip of grass. The place is new; New Place, they call it. He is planning the Knotte Garden. Shall there be wild-flowers in it? Mary-buds, by all means. They will gather harebells soon. Some say they were left, like the rosemary-dust that powders his woven-wool shawl, by the Conqueror. *Let Rome in Tiber melt—here is my—here is my—* But we are thinking of the Knotte Garden. How design it? Judith has gone away. Now where is Hamnet? *To-morrow and to-morrow and to-morrow. Out, out brief candle.* But it was not very brief. There were long waits between. *From you have I been absent in the spring.* Not this spring, certainly.

When daisies pied and violets blue,
And lady-smocks all silver-white,
And cuckoo-buds of yellow hue
Do paint the meadows with delight . . .

But *white* and *delight* had happened before, and *hue* and *blue* everywhere. But *hue* was different, that time.

From you have I been absent in the spring,
When proud-pied April, dressed in all his trim—

but proud-pied—it was daisies pied, a moment ago. Pied? Dappled, two-coloured, part-coloured, two-souled. Where was the advantage in that, *O master-mistress of my passion?* It was *daisies smell-less but most quaint* now. He would no longer . . . *white—delight?*

Nor did I wonder at the lily's white
Nor praise the deep vermilion in the rose,
They were but sweet, but figures of delight,
Drawn after you, you pattern of all those.

But who was the pattern of all those? A child tugged at the knotted edge of his grey shawl. Another child was laughing, but it wasn't Hamnet. He looked at her–his face. They were both his children, but Judith with her hair tucked over her ears, was no Juliet. Judith was Hamnet. Hamnet was Judith. And he had left them at the bridge and spurred his horse through Oxford for an idle fantasy. Perfection dwelt in two separate. There was no *master-mistress of my passion*. It was late now. But Judith understood what he wanted with the garden.

Mary-buds begin
To ope their golden eyes.

Yes, marigolds. But king-cups were not suitable for the garden. Like deadmen's-fingers, they dug deep. Deadmen's-fingers? He had some time avoided their country name. The flowers grew on a long stem, more than half of which was white-green under the leaves. The flower resembled the harebell but was a different colour, blue and violet; he called them both long-purples.

But Mary-buds were closing. Was it evening? That bell, the misereri? *I am sick, I must die.*

The bells were from London.

Thomas Nash was born three years after Shakespeare. He died fifteen years earlier; he was thirty-four. Like Marlowe and Raleigh, his life was suspect. He had spent some time in prison. It was 1600, when he wrote *Summer's Last Will and Testament.* He died a year later.

Adieu, farewell earth's bliss!
This world uncertain is,
Fond are life's lustful joys,
Death proves them all but toys;
None from his darts can fly:
I am sick, I must die,
Lord have mercy on us!

Rich men, trust not in wealth,
Gold can not buy you health;
Physic himself must fade;
All things to end are made;
The plague full swift goes by;
I am sick, I must die.
Lord have mercy on us!

Beauty is but a flower,
Which wrinkles will devour:
Brightness falls from the air;
Queens have died young and fair;
Dust hath closed Helen's eye;
I am sick, I must die.
Lord have mercy on us!

Strength stoops unto the grave:
Worms feed on Hector brave;
Swords may not fight with fate:
Earth still holds ope her gate.
Come, come, the bells do cry;
I am sick, I must die.
Lord have mercy on us!

Wit with his wantonness,
Tasteth death's bitterness,
Hell's executioner

Hath no ears for to hear
What vain art can reply;
I am sick, I must die.
Lord have mercy on us!

Haste therefore each degree
To welcome destiny:
Heaven is our heritage,
Earth but a player's stage,
Mount we unto the sky;
I am sick, I must die.
Lord have mercy on us!

Thomas Nash is known as the companion of Robert Greene, George Peele and Christopher Marlowe. Robert Greene, his inseparable companion, was seven years older and died nine years earlier, again suspect. They were possibly all secret-service agents. Accomplished scholars, Nash and Greene like Marlowe had travelled widely in France and Italy. Nash, we may conclude, died of the plague. Robert Greene escaped it by some eight years. His death, like Marlowe's, however, has remained a mystery. George Peele lived to the age of forty. He, too, is accused of haunting low river-side taverns and even, indirectly, of having met his death in one of them, possibly by poisoning. Marlowe's exploits are apt, in popular esteem, to overshadow the careers of the less robust members of, possibly, a sort of secret-service group working in the service of the Queen, probably working dangerously as counter-espionage agents.

But their lives like their deaths are overshadowed by that other agent of Queen Elizabeth. Sir Walter Raleigh was only twelve years older than the most important member of this group. Christopher Marlowe died at twenty-nine. Raleigh was sixty-six when he wrote, that last evening in the Tower:

Give me my scallop-shell of quiet,
My staff of faith to walk upon,

My scrip of joy, immortal diet,
  My bottle of salvation,
My gown of glory, hope's true gage;
And thus I'll take my pilgrimage.

Blood must be my body's balmer;
  No other balm will there be given;
Whilst my soul, like quiet palmer,
  Travelleth toward the land of heaven;
Over the silver mountains,
Where spring the nectar fountains.

        There will I kiss
        The bowl of bliss;
And drink mine everlasting fill
Upon every milken hill.
My soul will be a-dry before;
But after it will thirst no more.

Ben Jonson's name is bracketed, as a rule, with that of Michael Drayton and of Shakespeare. From Sir Walter Raleigh to Ben Jonson is an easy transition. They were both, taken all in all, solid men. Sir Walter of the Devonshire landed gentry looked out from Plymouth, toward more land. Ben Jonson, a Scotsman, traditionally of poor parents, born in London, sought to attain a lost inheritance. He wrote plays solely, he said, to gain a livelihood. He was eight years younger than Shakespeare and twenty years younger than Raleigh. Yet he seems, in a way, a bridge between these two. His was an old head on young shoulders, but he never, in any sense of the word, lost that head. We feel in some way, that there was no Mary Arden in his background.

There was, no doubt, a deposed Catholic mystic in Ben Jonson's make-up. It accounts for his processions of Queens, who might have been, in the earlier Tudor period, mediaeval saints. His majestic pageants were removed, however, from the real realm of fantasy; the people of his play were abstract. They were Virtues, for the most part, or Latinized figures from a Renaissance series, a wall-painting where Vanity is trod down by Modesty, and Rhetoric joins hands with Poetry. They are the images or abstractions of the humanists, gorgeously arrayed in folds of painted raiment. *Queen and Huntress, chaste and fair,* stands in white. She is this Cynthia of their eternal preoccupation. The mind of the Tudor Englishman could loyally transfer his ancestors' allegiance to the Queen of England. What the heart lost, the mind gained thereby.

We can not imagine Ben Jonson other than preoccupied with the classics. He was a bookish child, we may be sure of that, with few books. Books were the prized possession of aristocrats, for the most part, or were treasured in the small out-posts of monasticism, in and around London. We can imagine Ben Jonson bargaining with a Greyfriar. Tacitus and Livy, to us, are dry and lifeless; Plautus and Terence, worse. Yet Ben Jonson, I should imagine, would have given literally, his soul for more Latin and more Greek. The child at Avon, on the other hand, boasted in later life of other exploits. With moon-light on the snow, he sought the forest of Sir Thomas Lucy. Whose was the fairer Huntress? She, Cynthia, is said with her arrows, to give madness.

Michael Drayton was born the year before Shakespeare. Drayton was a Warwickshire lad. Drayton's name has been recorded with Ben Jonson's, in the notable page of a certain vicar of Stratford, who has gained immortality by a spiteful entry in his private diary. It was April, 1616, when William Shakespeare of New Place, thought wistfully of gilly-flowers, clove-pinks or, as some called them, sops-in-wine. There was to be a hedge of holly and someone would graft, he knew, low to the ground, to be the better seen there, a branch of mistletoe. Best graft it to the espalier, apple or pear or plum; fruit-wood would take mistletoe. *Blow, blow thou winter wind. Thou art not so unkind—* it was cold now.

This is the entry from the private diary: "Shakespeare, Drayton, and Ben Jonson had a merry meeting and it seems drank too hard, for Shakespeare died of a fever there contracted."

Michael Drayton is perhaps best remembered by his stirring ballad, *Agincourt.* Whether or not his King Henry was inspired by the "perfect King," the reprobate friend of Falstaff and Sir Pierce of Exton, turned reformer in *Henry V,* is beside the point.

Fair stood the wind for France
When we our sails advance
Nor now to prove our chance
  Longer will tarry;
But putting to the main,
At Caux, the mouth of Seine,
With all his martial train,
  Landed King Harry.

Upon Saint Crispin's Day
Fought was this noble fray,
Which fame did not delay
  To England to carry.
O when shall English men
With such acts fill a pen?
Or England breed again
  Such a King Harry?

Drayton's *Agincourt* stands by itself, with or without Shakespeare's *Henry V,* just as his *Virginian Voyage* will be remembered by many who have never heard of *Nymphi-*

dia, except as the original of Shakespeare's later Oberon and Queen Mab.

John Webster is admittedly one of the greatest of the English dramatists, yet the date of his birth is usually indicated by a question-mark. His death is given as 1630. Perhaps, in a way, this is significant, for Webster was obsessed with the mediaeval concept of death. With him, it is indeed *vanitas vanitatum.* He is concerned with unburied men as well as with buried ones. I myself would conclude that John Webster was fairly young at the time of the Great Plague. I believe he was at an exceptionally sensitive and impressionable age, when the plague swept London. We are given no indication of the place of his birth. Was he a London child, who was found destitute, beating his fists against a locked door—locked from without by the grim Watch? I imagine him somewhere near Saint Paul's. The plague-pits had destroyed his land-marks. It may have been a kindly Watch who locked him in.

His name is Webster, his name is John. He beats and beats on the firm oak, with his small fists. In the room behind him, lies one of whom he was later to write:

> Strew your hair with powders sweet
> Don clean linen, bathe your feet,
> And—the foul fiend more to check—
> A crucifix let bless your neck:
> 'Tis now full tide 'tween night and day;
> End your groan and come away.

But the groan had long since ended. He could only remember her concern. There was a faint fragrance lingering in the air, though the charcoal burner in the dark room behind him, had turned ash, two days ago. The tallow-dips had given out before that.

All the flowers of the spring
Meet to perfume our burying.

Thomas Dekker with Thomas Middleton was known to be a friend and collaborator of John Webster. Thomas Middleton again, has a question-mark after the date of his birth, though it is conjectured that he was born about 1570. Dekker's is also given as about 1570.

Logically then, we might reason that John Webster would be little more than thirty when the plague swept London. But again, we do not know where Webster was born. Thomas Dekker was "one of the celebrated wits of the reign of James I." Thomas Middleton "of whom little is known," becomes "Chronologer to the City of London shortly before his death." And John Webster himself, "a member of the Merchant Taylor's Company."

Substantial men, we might say, these three, or else favourites of a corrupt Court. I visualize Thomas Middleton as grey-haired and worthy of the honour bestowed shortly before his death. But perhaps Chronologer to me, conjures up an image of vast respectability, a reputable and not-too-old Father Time, in fact. But it is better to follow one's own clues and have of each of these poets, a living and personal memory, rather than grow weary and confused with disputable facts about them.

Thomas Middleton's dramas are drawn after the same grim pattern as Webster's most famous one, *The Duchess of Malfi*. If we are confused about Middleton's authenticity, it is no small wonder. Beside his own plays, he is known to have contributed whole scenes to well-known works of William Rowley, Philip Massinger, John Fletcher and Ben Jonson.

But the name of Thomas Dekker is lighted as by flambeaux: on the one hand, *Sweet Content,* on the other, *Sorrow.*

Art thou poor, yet hast thou golden slumbers?
  O sweet content!
Art thou rich, yet is thy mind perplex'd?
  O punishment!
Dost thou laugh to see how fools are vex't
To add to golden numbers golden numbers?
  O sweet content! O sweet, O sweet content!

Can'st drink the waters of the crispèd spring?
  O sweet content!
Swim'st thou in wealth, yet sink'st in thine own tears?
  O punishment!
Then he that patiently want's burden bears,
No burden bears, but is a king, a king!
  O sweet content! O sweet, O sweet content!

✣ ✣ ✣

O, Sorrow, Sorrow say where thou dost dwell?
  In the lowest room of Hell.
  Art thou born of human race?
  No, no, I have a furier face.
Art thou in city, town or court?
  I to every place resort.
O, why into the world is Sorrow sent?
  Men afflicted best repent.
    What dost thou feed on?
      Broken sleep.
  What takest thou pleasure in?
      To weep,
  To sigh, to sob, to pine, to groan,
  To wring my hands, to sit alone.
O when, O when shall Sorrow quiet have?
  Never, never, never, never,
  Never till she finds a grave.

As Thomas Middleton's exact value is difficult to assess, so to an even greater degree, is that of Philip Massinger.

Perhaps one line may better place him, than argument as to how much of his reputation is due to his intimate friendship with John Fletcher. It is enough that he stands by *The Blushing Rose and Purple Flower.* We do know that Philip Massinger "was at one time page in the household of the Earl of Pembroke," and that "some fifteen plays are to his credit."

We may judge that Philip Massinger was a later friend of John Fletcher. It must be remembered that it was Francis Beaumont who lured the older man into writing. John Fletcher was five years older than Francis Beaumont, and we may wonder what terror or superstition kept Fletcher's imagination tied down, dispersed or in prison, during those earlier years. Why did he not write sooner? Or why did he write at all? As it happens, the name John Fletcher now takes precedence of that of his generous patron, the younger brother of Sir John Beaumont, who was himself a poet. John Fletcher collaborated, it is true, with Philip Massinger but it was possibly the death of his friend, Beaumont, that caused him to seek a substitute for that loss. "Also attributed to William Shakespeare" has been frequently written after John Fletcher's name.

Beaumont, his intimate friend, and William Shakespeare both died in 1616.

Roses, their sharp spines being gone,
Not royal in their smells alone,
    But in their hue;
Maiden pinks, of odour faint,
Daisies smell-less, yet most quaint,
    And sweet thyme true;

Primrose, first-born child of Ver;
Merry spring-time's harbinger,
    With hare-bells dim;
Oxlips in their cradles growing,

Marigolds on death-beds blowing,
   Larks'-heels trim.

All dear Nature's children sweet
Lie 'fore bride and bridegroom's feet,
   Blessing their sense!
Not an angel of the air,
Bird melodious, or bird fair,
   Be absent hence!

The crow, the slanderous cuckoo, nor
The boding raven, nor chough hoar,
   Nor chattering pye,
May on our bride house perch or sing,
Or with them any discord bring,
   But from it fly!

Francis Beaumont was thirty-two years old when he died. Shakespeare was fifty-two. John Fletcher lived nine years longer. He attained the unique honour, among the one hundred lyric poets, roughly attributed to the Elizabethan age, of being, from time to time, confused with William Shakespeare. There are many lyrics of Shakespeare's which might well be attributed to Fletcher, who was only fifteen years younger. We wonder where it was that the son of Richard Fletcher, the future Bishop of London, and the then not so famous rival of Christopher Marlowe, first met. Gentle Shakespeare is so common a phrase that we have ceased to think about it. But the word, gentle, seems equally appropriate to the retiring scholar, John Fletcher, who needed the more robust young aristocrat, Francis Beaumont, to give him the assurance that perhaps, the gentle Shakespeare also lacked. We have come back to Court with Pembroke's page, Philip Massinger and with the brother of Sir John Beaumont.

The son of the then obscure Richard Fletcher and the grammar school boy from Stratford did not feel at home there.

As to Francis Beaumont, it is he, in retrospect, whose important name becomes a shadow. *Luce's Dirge* from *The Knight of the Burning Pestle,* might have been written by either John Fletcher or William Shakespeare.

Come, you whose loves are dead,
  And, whiles I sing,
    Weep and wring
Every hand, and every head
Bind with cypress and sad yew;
Ribbons black and candles blue
For him that was of men most true!

Come with heavy moaning,
  And on his grave
  Let him have
Sacrifice of sighs and groaning;
Let him have fair flowers enow,
White and purple, green and yellow,
For him that was of men most true!

And yet, on reconsideration, there seems a distinctly un-Fletcherian flavour about the light touch. No doubt, some sort of *Dirge* was necessary, at this moment, for the occult disasters, attendant on the bold experiments with crucible and astrolabe. There was the historical precedent of the sudden leap to fame and the more precipitate fall to infamy, of Doctor John Dee. But we do not feel that Francis Beaumont was in any way involved with the philosopher's stone or the transmutation of base metal into gold. The Queen had been dead ten years when the two of them put the finishing touches to *The Knight.* It was no longer necessary to follow the vagaries of the Court—or at least now, there were other fashions at the Court of King James. Francis Beaumont we feel, in any case, was an independent entity. This poem shows it. With a delicate yet robust touch, he strives for something different. He is not great enough to be trivial. He would never fill in a line with so immature a device as *lulla, lulla, lullaby* or:

> Then heigh ho, the holly:
> This life is most jolly.

I have said that *Luce's Dirge* might have been written by Beaumont's collaborator, John Fletcher or by Shakespeare. I was wrong. There is not Fletcher's even temper in it. There is not Shakespeare's indifference to originality. *Out, out brief candle* could never have been blue, and flowers, *white and purple, green and yellow* would have been, by no alchemy, but by a simple process of association, *daisies pied and violets blue* or else *the marigold that goes to bed with the sun.*

If we conclude that John Webster was roughly a contemporary of his collaborators, Middleton and Dekker, we realize that the date of his birth was probably within less than a decade of that of John Donne. Certainly, Webster and Donne had much in common, chiefly the terror of death. If Thomas Nash gives us

> Come, come the bells do cry;
> I am sick, I must die,

we must conclude that his contemporaries were obsessed with the same prescience. Thomas Nash, it is generally believed, died of the plague in 1601. The others, whose ages varied, were none the less, living under the same conditions. John Donne, at any rate, went through some startling transformations. From the strong Catholicism of his mother and probably of his childhood, he turned to an exaltation of the flesh. But this is the same John Donne who in his more solid middle-years proclaimed from the pulpit of Saint Paul's his doctrine of the body's dissolution. His gruesome classics are unparalleled in their minute details of physical disintegration; he invokes and almost conjures out of the tomb, for our precise edification, the decayed or worse, decaying and cast-off garment of the soul. His sermons were all of death, but like John Webster, it is the death of the body that obsessed him. We have visualized John Webster as a child. I see John Donne at some period of his youth in monastic garb, one of a procession with charcoal sticks, dried herbs and pick and spade.

The *Dirge* of Francis Beaumont which we have just quoted, like the exquisite lines sung by the fool in *Twelfth Night,* have (for all of *poor corse* and *bones*), nothing of death about them.

> Come away, come away, death,
> And in sad cypress let me be laid;
> Fly away, fly away, breath;
> I am slain by a fair cruel maid.
> My shroud of white, stuck all with yew,
> O prepare it!
> My part of death, no one so true
> Did share it.
>
> Not a flower, not a flower sweet,
> On my black coffin let there be strown;
> Not a friend, not a friend greet
> My poor corse, where my bones shall be thrown:
> A thousand thousand sighs to save,
> Lay me, O, where
> Sad true lover never find my grave
> To weep there!

Richard Crashaw comes somewhat later. He was born in 1613, three years before the death of Shakespeare. His early lyrics follow the pattern of *Supposed Mistress* and *Shepherd's Hymn.* But his youthful conflicts are soon settled by full allegiance to Rome. A favourite of Queen

Henrietta Maria, "he died soon after he became beneficiary of the Basilica Church of Our Lady of Loreto." His poem to Saint Teresa contains some of the most luminous and ecstatic lines in English poetry.

> Love, thou art absolute, sole Lord
> Of life and death.

The Flaming Heart is dedicated to the Saint of Avila. Teresa with Seraph and darts, has usurped the place of the earlier Love with his arrows. The poet, like the Saint, has transferred his allegiance from earthly martyrdom to heavenly. Love is, in any case, a martyrdom. It still remains a question, however, whether the poet in retreat at Loreto, was by that "beneficiary," the greater martyr than the tortured being who in 1600, cried out

> Haste therefore each degree
> To welcome destiny.

Thomas Nash, we may presume, might also have found refuge in a monastery. The same might be said of any of his contemporaries. Some may have taken refuge in the country, others may have wished to return to London, but have been refused admittance. In any case, the mark of the plague was on them.

There is no doubt, however, that the "beneficiary" made the greater poet of Richard Crashaw.

> Live in these conquering leaves: live all the same;
> And walk through all tongues one triumphant flame;
> Live here, great heart; and love and die and kill;
> And bleed, and wound, and yield, and conquer still.
> Let this immortal life where'er it comes
> Walk in a crowd of loves and martyrdoms.
> Let mystic death wait on't; and wise souls be
> The love-slain witness of this life of thee.
> O sweet incendiary! show here thy art,
> Upon this carcass of a hard cold heart;

Let all thy scattered shafts of light, that play
Among the leaves of thy large books of day,
Combined against this breast at once break in,
And take away from me my self and sin.

There was no religious conflict in George Herbert. The younger man escaped the divided allegiance of John Donne. The court bestowed on this younger brother of the poet, Edward, Lord Herbert of Cherbury, no "beneficiary." This "pure and saint-like" being took over the modest living of an English country parish. Yet in the cool recess of that remote place, he produced sonorous, ritualistic poetry which rivalled that of the Roman convert at Loreto and the still Romanized Dean of Saint Paul's.

I struck the board and cried, No more;
I will abroad.
What, shall I ever sigh and pine?
My lines and life are free, free as the road,
Loose as the wind, as large as store.
  Shall I be still in suit?
Have I no harvest but a thorn
To let me blood, and not restore
What I have lost with cordial fruit?
  Sure there was wine
Before my sighs did dry it; there was corn
Before my tears did drown it.
Is the year only lost to me?
Have I no bays to crown it?
No flowers, no garlands gay? All blasted?
  All wasted?
Not so, my heart; but there is fruit,
  And thou hast hands.
Recover all thy sigh-blown age
On double pleasures; leave thy cold dispute
Of what is fit and not; forsake thy cage,

Thy rope of sands
Which petty thoughts have made, and made to thee
Good cable to enforce and draw
And be thy law,
While thou didst wink and wouldst not see.
Away: take heed,
I will abroad.
Call in thy death's-head there: tie up thy fears.
He that forbears
To suit and serve his need
Deserves his load.
But as I raved and grew more fierce and wild
At every word,
Methought I heard one calling, *'Child!'*
And I replied *'My Lord!'*

John Ford was a little older than George Herbert. Although he stands high in the ranks of post-Shakespearian dramatists, I personally prefer him because he is said to have written the music for *Guests.* This exquisite poem might have been written by George Herbert, although it appears in the later editions of Elizabethan Song Books, as Anonymous or is labelled simply, Christ Church MS. It would seem for this reason, to belong to an earlier period, but the sentiment is wholly of the later group, the so-called post-Shakespearian lyrists, who were born toward the end of the sixteenth century.

Yet if His Majesty, our sovereign lord,
Should of his own accord,
Friendly himself invite,
And say, 'I'll be your guest to-morrow night,'
How should we stir ourselves, call and command
All hands to work! 'Let no man idle stand.

'Set me fine Spanish tables in the hall,
See they be fitted all;

Let there be room to eat,
And order taken that there want no meat.
See every sconce and candlestick made bright,
That without tapers they may give a light.

'Look to the presence; are the carpets spread,
The dazie o'er the head,
The cushions in the chairs,
And all the candles lighted on the stairs?
Perfume the chambers, and in any case
Let each man give attendance in his place.'

Thus, if the king were coming, would we do,
And 'twere good reason too;
For 'tis a duteous thing
To show all honour to an earthly king,
And after all our travail and our cost,
So he be pleased, to think no labour lost.

But at the coming of the King of Heaven
All's set at six and seven:
We wallow in our sin,
Christ can not find a chamber in the inn.
We entertain him always like a stranger,
And, as at first, still lodge Him in the manger.

Richard Rowland's *Our Blessed Lady's Lullaby,* by the merest chance, is not anonymous. He too is associated with Christ Church College, Oxford, and it might be even more apposite to say that he might have written *Guests.* He was born the same year or the year after Shakespeare, but, an ardent Catholic, he left Oxford, set up a press in Antwerp and took the name of his Dutch grandfather. The English Jesuit, Robert Southwell was born a few years earlier. He returned to England, after some years as Prefect in Rome.

He died a martyr at Tyburn, 1595, after an imprisonment of three years. *The Burning Babe* caused Ben Jonson to say, "he would have been content to destroy his own writings if he would have written this poem."

As I in hoary winter's night
  Stood shivering in the snow
Surprised was I with sudden heat
  Which made my heart to glow;
And lifting up a fearful eye
  To view what fire was near,
A pretty babe all burning bright
  Did in the air appear.

✣ ✣ ✣

With this He vanish'd out of sight
  And swiftly shrunk away,
And straight I callèd unto mind
  That it was Christmas Day.

Francis Quarles, also of Christ Church, though somewhat later, was another martyr. He was cupbearer to that same Elizabeth of Bohemia, for whom Shakespeare wrote *The Tempest.* Later, the Commonwealth took his estate, but what "sent him to his grave" was the sacrilege committed on his books.

My soul, sit thou a patient looker-on;
Judge not the play before the play is done:
Her plot has many changes; every day
Speaks a new scene; the last act crowns the play.

Of William Strode we know nothing whatever, except that he was a contemporary of Francis Quarles. His *Music,* however, gives him a place with this group.

O, lull me, lull me, charming air!
  My senses rock with wonder sweet;
Like snow on wool thy fallings are;
  Soft like a spirit's are thy feet!
    Grief who need fear

That hath an ear?
Down let him lie,
And slumbering die,
And change his soul for harmony.

Sir John Beaumont, Francis Beaumont's older brother, is usually neglected because of the younger man's affiliation with John Fletcher and hence, by association, with Shakespeare. But John Beaumont's *Of His Dear Son, Gervase* belongs to the devotional poetry of this time.

Dear Lord, receive my son, whose winning love
To me was like a friendship, far above
The course of nature or his tender age;
Whose looks could all my bitter griefs assuage;
Let his pure soul, ordained seven years to be
In that frail body which was part of me,
Remain my pledge in Heaven, as sent to show
How to this port at every step I go.

Phineas Fletcher, like John Beaumont, is apt to be ignored, because of his older cousin. His lyric however, *Drop, drop slow tears* must not be forgotten.

Drop, drop slow tears,
And bathe those beauteous feet
Which brought from Heaven
The news and Prince of Peace:
Cease not, wet eyes,
His mercies to entreat:
To cry for vengeance
Sin doth never cease.
In your deep floods
Drown all my faults and fears;
Nor let His eye
See sin, but through my tears.

His brother, Giles Fletcher, was even less fortunate. He took orders but was said to have died of grief because of the lack of sympathy shown him by his parishioners.

It was to Drummond of Hawthornden that Ben Jonson said that he would rather have written the one poem, *The Burning Babe,* than have produced all his own elaborate and beautiful Pageants and Masques. William Drummond was a Scotsman like himself. Drummond's sonnets are supposed to be among the best in the language. Personally, though William Drummond is not classed among the purely religious or devotional poets, I prefer his sonnet sequence, *Flowers of Sion.* John the Baptist cries out:

> 'All ye whose hopes rely
> On God, with me amidst these deserts mourn;
> Repent, repent, and from old errors turn!'
> —Who listen'd to his voice, obey'd his cry?
> Only the echoes, which he made relent,
> Rung from their flinty caves, *'Repent! Repent!'*

Henry King, Bishop of Chichester, was also a friend of Ben Jonson's and a conventional writer of sonnets. But perhaps he is best represented by his *Exequy:*

> Sleep on, my Love, in thy cold bed
> Never to be disquieted!

James Shirley belongs to this group of religious writers. George Herbert was born in 1593, James Shirley in 1596. Shirley was also intended for the Church, but he avoided exile from court and city. *Is the year only lost to me?* cries George Herbert from his country parish. But James Shirley capitulated. Rome and Queen Henrietta Maria claimed him. He was "the last of the great group of dramatists who immediately followed Shakespeare." But conflict must have run in the blood of this Englishman, for he does not attain the unity either of Richard Crashaw at Loreto, nor that of George Herbert in his country parish.

> The glories of our blood and state
> Are shadows, not substantial things;
> There is no armour against Fate;

Death lays his icy hand on kings:
Sceptre and Crown
Must tumble down,
And in the dust be equal made
With the poor crooked scythe and spade.

Some men with swords may reap the field,
And plant fresh laurels where they kill:
But their strong nerves at last must yield;
They tame but one another still:
Early or late
They stoop to fate,
And must give up their murmuring breath
When they, pale captives, creep to death.

The garlands wither on your brow;
Then boast no more your mighty deeds;
Upon Death's purple altar now
See where the victor-victim bleeds.
Your heads must come
To the cold tomb;
Only the actions of the just
Smell sweet and blossom in their dust.

Although Robert Herrick unquestionably belongs to this group, the son of the prosperous London goldsmith seems to have had no religious conflicts of any sort. Like George Herbert, his early lyrics were written from a country parish, but there is no hue and cry:

Away: take heed,
I will abroad.

Robert Herrick was quite content at Dean Prior, Devonshire. We may imagine the young bachelor riding in leisurely manner, through those fields.

Fair daffodils we weep to see
  You haste away so soon;
As yet the early-rising sun
  Has not attain'd his noon.
    Stay, stay
    Until the hasting day
                Has run
    But to the evensong;
And having prayed together, we
Will go with you along.

He has time and leisure and attractive duties. The country has not yet been ravaged by death. Robert Herrick travels out of his parish, but not far. There are violets growing along the hollows.

Welcome, maids of honour,
  You do bring
  In the Spring
And wait upon her.

She has virgins many,
  Fresh and fair;
  Yet you are
More sweet than any.

You're the maiden posies,
  And so graced
  To be placed
'Fore damask roses.

Yet, though thus respected,
  By-and-by
  Ye do die,
Poor girls neglected.

But there are other girls who must not be neglected. They are the daughters of the princely Manor Houses within the circuit of a day's ride. Their sympathies are naturally with the Court, but Robert Herrick out-does Pembroke's page and Sir John Beaumont's brother, in knowledge of the world. If he neglects Julia, she will recover. It is true, Electra, Œnone and Anthea may command him anything. In the end, they do command him. He takes his stand with the Royalists.

> Bid me to live, and I will live
> Thy Protestant to be;
> Or bid me love and I will give
> A loving heart to thee.

For his Royalist sympathies, he is ejected from his parish and returns to London. For years, we hear nothing of him. James, Charles, the Commonwealth and Charles II follow one another. But where is Robert Herrick?

Sir Walter Raleigh hurled his invective at the Court of King James:

> Say to the Court, it glows
> And shines like rotten wood.

Shakespeare retired to Stratford. In the character of Prospero, he confesses in the Epilogue to *The Tempest:*

> Now my charms are all o'erthrown,
> And what strength I have's mine own.

It is generally accepted that this play was written as Shakespeare's farewell to Court. In it, however, there is no hint of bitterness or rivalry. If he is to be elbowed out, he will at least, give at the last, a demonstration of good manners. Robert Herrick has never been compared to Shakespeare, and there was no question of rivalry or competition. Actually, most of his poems appeared anonymously. It was only in later life, that he himself collected them. He was almost sixty, when he issued his own poems, under the title *Hesperides.*

Robert Herrick lived to the age of eighty-three. He was

restored to his Devonshire parish two years after the return of Charles II. He was then seventy-one.

Two names are inevitably associated with that of Robert Herrick.

> Bid me to live and I will live
> Thy Protestant to be

is repeated, a theme with variations, by Richard Lovelace and by Edmund Waller. It is true that these lesser poets were born some time after the death of Elizabeth, but they reflect Sir Philip Sidney and Robert Herrick, without imitating them. Richard Lovelace, in a marked degree, suggests Robert Herrick, in his *Althea from Prison* and his *Lucasta* poems. The very names might have been of Herrick's choosing, and yet the familiar lines are his own.

> Tell me not, Sweet, I am unkind
> That from the nunnery
> Of thy chaste breast and quiet mind
> To war and arms I fly.
>
> True, a new mistress now I chase,
> The first foe in the field;
> And with a stronger faith embrace
> A sword, a horse, a shield.
>
> Yet this inconstancy is such
> As you too shall adore;
> I could not love thee, Dear, so much
> Loved I not Honour more.

Edmund Waller was likewise imprisoned during the wars. His name and reputation, like that of Richard Lovelace, rest solely on one poem.

> Go, lovely Rose—
> Tell her that wastes her time and me,

That now she knows,
When I resemble her to thee,
How sweet and fair she seems to be.

Tell her that's young,
And shuns to have her graces spied,
That hadst thou sprung
In deserts where no men abide,
Thou must have uncommended died.

Small is the worth
Of beauty from the light retired:
Bid her come forth,
Suffer herself to be desired,
And not blush so to be admired.

Then die—that she
The common fate of all things rare
May read in thee;
How small a part of time they share
That are so wondrous sweet and fair.

As a contrast to Lovelace and Waller, there is Sir John Suckling. He joined the army of Gustavus Adolphus, returned with one hundred horse and fought with the Scotch and Royalists. His career was one of "wild and reckless dissipation" and it is said, "fleeing from England, he put an end to his life in Paris." His life and poetry are the reverse of

Bid me to live and I will live
Thy Protestant to be,

and

I could not love thee, Dear, so much
Loved I not Honour more.

Of Love and Honour, he wrote:

Some bays, perchance, or myrtle bough
For difference crowns the brow

Of those kind souls that were
The noble martyrs here:
And if that be the only odds
(As who can tell?), ye kinder gods,
Give me the woman here!

His friend, Thomas Carew, cupbearer to Charles I, however, though reported to be "fonder of roving after hounds and hawks" than of plays and poetry, yet contradicts this with his exquisite *Song:*

Ask me no more where Jove bestows,
When June is past, the fading rose;
For in your beauty's orient deep
These flowers, as in their causes, sleep.

Ask me no more if east or west
The Phoenix builds her spicy nest;
For unto you at last, she flies,
And in your fragrant bosom dies.

Henry Constable was about Shakespeare's age. His lyrics, notably *Diaphenia,* appear in various song books.

Diaphenia, like to all things blessèd
When all thy praises are expressèd,
Dear joy, how I do love thee!
As the birds do love the spring,
Or the bees their careful king:
Then in requite, sweet virgin, love me!

Sir William Davenant, a reputed godson of Shakespeare, was a friend of the king's cupbearer, Thomas Carew and the "wild and reckless" Sir John Suckling. He is best known by his *Song:*

The lark now leaves his wat'ry nest,
And climbing, shakes his dewy wings.
He takes this window for the East,
And to implore your light he sings—

Awake, awake! the morn will never rise
Till she can dress her beauty at your eyes.

Sir Henry Wotton, born four years after Shakespeare, again owes his reputation to one poem. He had travelled in France and Italy on various diplomatic missions, during the reign of Queen Elizabeth. Venice and the German states claimed him, when James became king. *The Tempest* was written to celebrate the marriage of James' daughter, Elizabeth, later known as Elizabeth of Bohemia or the Winter Queen. It was to this unfortunate princess that Wotton in later years, dedicated his life.

You meaner beauties of the night,
  That poorly satisfy our eyes
More by your number than your light,
  You common people of the skies;
What are you when the moon shall rise?

You curious chanters of the wood,
  That warble forth Dame Nature's lays,
Thinking your passions understood
  By your weak accents; what's your praise
When Philomel her voice shall raise?

You violets that first appear,
  By your pure purple mantles known
Like the proud virgins of the year,
  As if the spring were all your own;
What are you when the rose is blown?

So, when my mistress shall be seen
  In form and beauty of her mind,
By virtue first, then choice, a Queen,
  Tell me, if she were not designed
Th' eclipse and glory of her kind.

Another Elizabeth recalls a like devotion. The unfortunate favourite, Robert Devereux was beheaded, like Raleigh. The Earl of Essex was only thirty-four at the time of his death. *A Passion of My Lord of Essex* was enclosed in a letter from Ireland, to the Queen. This other "passion" might well have been indited from the Tower, as was Raleigh's *Go, Soul, the Body's guest.*

Her thoughts and mine such disproportion have;
All strength of Love is infinite in me;
She useth the 'vantage time and fortune gave
Of worth and power to get the liberty.
Earth, sea, heaven, hell, are subject unto laws,
But I, poor I, must suffer and know no cause.

Francis Davison escaped death at the beginning of the reign of Elizabeth, but he was "disgraced for carrying her warrant for execution of Mary Stuart to the Council." *My only star* might have been written by Essex from the Tower.

O cruel tiger!
If to your hard heart's center
Tears, vows, and prayers may enter,
Desist your rigour;
And let kind lines assure me,
Since to my deadly wound
No salve else can be found,
That you that kill me, yet at length will cure me.

Essex was executed two years before the Queen's death. Seventeen years later, two years after the death of Shakespeare, Sir Walter Raleigh will feverishly conclude:

So when thou hast, as I
Commanded thee, done blabbing,—
Although to give the lie
Deserves no less than stabbing,—
Yet stab at thee that will,
No stab the soul can kill!

With Thomas Campion, we return to Paradise. He was born three years after Shakespeare and died four years after. He is classed with Herrick and Shakespeare as one of the three outstanding English lyric poets of all time. His words like Herrick's and Shakespeare's, sing themselves, yet in Campion's case, we possess the actual Song Books or Books of Aires, with the words and music, running along together, both written by the poet. It is possible that Thomas Campion wrote many of the airs for Shakespeare's lyrics. He, like Ben Jonson, follows the classic tradition. Few realize that Ben Jonson's familiar *Drink to me only with thine eyes* is a transcription from the Greek. It is possible that this familiar melody was written by Thomas Campion.

Perhaps Campion's most successful Latin rendering is that of Catullus' *Vivamus mea Lesbia, atque amemus.* Yet the darkness of the Latin poet's hopelessness in the face of death, is somehow turned to light, when Thomas Campion translates:

> But, soon as once set is our little light,
> Then must we sleep one ever-during night.

The same thing may be said of *In imagine pertransit homo.*

> Follow thy fair sun, unhappy shadow!
> Though thou be black as night,
> And she made all of light,
> Yet follow thy fair sun, unhappy shadow!
>
> Follow her, whose light thy light depriveth!
> Though here thou liv'st disgraced,
> And she in heaven is placed,
> Yet follow her whose light the world reviveth!
>
> Follow her, while yet her glory shineth!
> There comes a luckless night
> That will dim all her light;
> And this the black unhappy shade divineth.

Follow still, since so thy fates ordainèd!
The sun must have his shade,
Till both at once do fade;
The sun still proved, the shadow still disdainèd.

George Chapman belongs to the more conventional school of classic tradition. He is, of course, best known for his translation of Homer. He completed the *Hero and Leander,* left unfinished by Christopher Marlowe. He was born five years before Marlowe and Shakespeare. The song, *Muses that Sing* might have been written by George Chapman for one of the unfinished *Hero and Leander* sections.

Abjure those joys, abhor their memory,
And let my Love the honoured subject be
Of Love, and honour's complete history;
Your eyes were never yet let in to see
The majesty and riches of the mind,
But dwell in darkness; for your god is blind.

For your god is blind can not be said of Thomas Campion.

Follow still, since so thy fates ordainèd!
The sun must have his shade,
Till both at once do fade;
The sun still proved, the shadow still disdainèd.

For through the words, there is a lyric pulse that transmutes the mere syllables into a universal language. The sun and shadow merge. The eternal symbol of union becomes a sound of silver rain, as a light hand completes the stanza with a run of improvised notes, not contained in the original Book of Aires. The Paradise of Dante was actually the property of the humanists. The inspirational tenderness of *Come away, come away, Death* and *Fair Daffodils, we weep to see* transcends the death which they invoke. With Marlowe and Sir Walter Raleigh, there is death indeed, in spite of heroic defiance:

Yet stab at thee that will,
No stab the soul can kill!

Shakespeare, Campion and Robert Herrick do not need Dante's geometric circle within circle, to show the way from Hell to Paradise. If Hell was implicit in court and city, there were flowers to sweeten the stench of death. There were flowers to heal and flowers to be *strown . . . on my black coffin.* For these three, the lead that enclosed the body of the fortunate, was of no importance. *Come, come, the bells do cry, I am sick I must die* recalled other memory than that of the Black Watch.

Christopher Marlowe of "the mighty line" was undoubtedly an actor. He was *Tamburlaine the Great* and *Doctor Faustus.*

Is this the face that launched a thousand ships,
And burnt the topless towers of Ilium

is spoken aloud. It is declaimed in public or in the semi-privacy of a suspect tavern, with full knowledge of the ash upon the hearth-stone, the empty jug on the table and the crooked slant of an ill-fitting shutter. If there was no one to listen, still Kit Marlowe would declaim to the empty bench, drawn up before the ale-drenched table. *Helen make me immortal with a kiss* could be spoken to the dark wench who ordered him to bed, or to the lad who waited for the wits and gallants after the play, to scatter orange peel, so that he might have the possible chance of half an orange or the luck to find a loose coin in the strewn rush. Christopher Marlowe is known as "the first great dramatist in English literature." He is said to have influenced Shakespeare in his early plays. But Shakespeare as an actor in the Blackfriars Playhouse accepts only minor roles, or later, you might say, no role at all, as the ghost in *Hamlet* or Adam, Orlando's old retainer in *As You Like It.* We can not imagine the swash-buckling Marlowe, if he had appeared at all, accepting other than the main role. But Marlowe acted himself to death and so did Walter Raleigh.

But music like dream, transcends time and space. Marlowe's *The Jew of Malta* and *Edward II* recall *The Merchant of Venice* and the pageant of kings, *John, Richard II, Richard III, Henry IV* and *Henry V*. Through them, another, from a less illustrious town than Canterbury, pleads for an island.

> This royal throne of kings, this scepter'd isle,
> This earth of majesty, this seat of Mars,
> This other-Eden, demi-paradise,
> This fortress built by Nature for herself
> Against infection and the hand of war,
> This happy breed of men, this little world,
> This precious stone set in the silver sea,
> Which serves it in the office of a wall
> Or as a moat defensive to a house,
> Against the envy of less happier lands,
> This blessèd plot, this earth, this realm, this England.

But when infection had completed its devastation and when this throne of kings was no longer royal, William Shakespeare, unlike Christopher Marlowe, unlike Walter Raleigh, stands aside. We can not imagine him shut up in the Tower, and if accusation was brought against him, it was merely of "a merry meeting" and "fever there contracted." Thomas Campion lived to be almost exactly the same age, and Robert Herrick may be said, in his own person, to have prolonged the Elizabethan age, on through what later critics call the Jacobean, the Caroline, the Commonwealth and the Restoration. He died at the age of eighty-three, toward the end of the seventeenth century.

It may be noted that we have touched on the poetry of the minor Royalist poets, Lovelace, Waller, Suckling and Thomas Carew, and have not even mentioned the giant

Commonwealth or Puritan poet, John Milton. It has been contended that his muse is not Elizabethan, but it is not for that reason that we have been forced to exclude him. He stands alone, we do not even compare these lesser poets with him, nor is there any minor constellation to reflect his light. The inclusion of John Milton would unbalance this sequence and if we included him, we would exclude the others. It has been our intention to recall echoes of the great period by way of its minor satellites, rather than the heroic verse of this outstanding figure.

John Lyly is another of the great group. *Euphues* is remembered because of *euphuism*, a word coined from the name of the hero of Lyly's extravagant *Anatomy of Wit*. It is said that both Shakespeare and Ben Jonson wrote parodies on Lyly and his intention to re-make the English language. We find Shakespeare's parody in *Love's Labour's Lost* and Jonson's in *Every Man Out of His Humour*. But John Lyly, the poet lives, though Lyly the exponent of rhetoric, is shelved and un-read save by experts and historians.

What bird so sings, yet so does wail?
O 'tis the ravished nightingale.
Jug, jug, jug, jug, tereu! she cries,
And still her woes at midnight rise.
Brave prick-song! Who is't now we hear?
None but the lark so shrill and clear;
How at heaven's gate she claps her wings,
The morn not waking till she sings.
Hark, hark, with what a pretty throat
Poor robin redbreast tunes his note;
Hark how the jolly cuckoos sing
Cuckoo! to welcome in the spring!
Cuckoo! to welcome in the spring!

Thomas Heywood is reputed to be the author of two hundred and twenty plays, of which only twenty-three have survived. He dealt chiefly with country scenes and country people.

Pack clouds, away, and welcome day!
  With night we banish sorrow.
Sweet air, blow soft; mount, lark, aloft
  To give my Love good-morrow!
Wings from the wind to please her mind,
  Notes from the lark I'll borrow;
Bird, prune thy wing, nightingale, sing:
  To give my Love good-morrow!
  To give my Love good-morrow!
    Notes from them all I'll borrow.

Francis Bacon, like John Lyly, was steeped in the policies and politics of the time. He has been called one of the greatest of philosophers. He wrote essays, *Counsels, Civil and Moral,* the *Advancement of Learning,* and a translation of *De Augmentis Scientiarum.* The following poem is a transcription from the Greek.

The world's a bubble; and the life of Man
  Less than a span:
In his conception wretched—from the womb
  So to the tomb!
Curst from his cradle, and brought up to years
  With cares and fears.
Who then to frail mortality shall trust
But limns on water, or but writes in dust.

Our own affection still at home to please,
  Is a disease;
To cross the sea to any foreign soil,
  Peril and toil;
Wars with their noise affright us; when they cease
  We're worse in peace.
What then remains, but that we still should cry
For being born, or, being born, to die?

This is one theme of the Elizabethan age. Webster and Middleton are outstanding examples of the black wave of terror and depression that swept over the island, as a result of the dissolution of the monasteries and the seven years, spent by Mary in seeking to restore them. Following the fires of martyrdom and the reeking stench of the unburied, was an aftermath or after-birth of Hell. I have spoken of Dante. Webster, Middleton, Nash, Lodge, Donne plunged lower into the *Inferno*. There was a *Purgatorio,* however, implicit in the *Duchess of Malfi* and a *Mad World my Masters*. Dante, like Sophocles, drew on the abstract. Webster, Middleton, Dekker, Ford, Massinger and a host of others, portrayed, in a renaissance setting, parables that represented unbearable actuality. What they themselves had not seen, was common gossip of the older generation. From this mad world, there was no escape.

There was one escape. Dante found it in a dream. But Dante's dream is un-dreamlike in texture. He may have heard the bells of *Santa Maria Maggiore* or the *Trinita,* above the bridge, where he stood and saw the uncovered bier of a stranger, unveiled like the Simonetta of Botticelli. Or he may have followed the funeral procession of a girl, known to him personally. The girl, in any case, remains an abstraction, a myth. But with Webster, the girl is, as I have said, someone known intimately. If her face is uncovered, it is better that we hide our eyes and summon the young monk who loiters behind the others. His name is John Donne.

Of necessity, he with pick and spade, must consider this *poor corse.*

> Where I am clad in black,
> The token of my wrack,

writes Thomas Lodge. He is of this period.

> After death, when we are gone,
> Joy and pleasure is there none.

Thomas Lodge, the physician, may be classed with John Donne. If help came at all, it was usually too late. And the love of the humanitarian and the healer breaks before the sight of endless agony and piteous decay.

Accurst be Love, and those that trust his trains!
He seemeth blind, yet wounds with art,
He sows content, he pays with smart,
He swears relief, yet kills the heart,
He calls for truth, yet scorns desart.
Accurst be Love, and those that trust his trains!
Whose heaven is hell, whose perfect joys are pains.

I have mentioned Sir Edward Dyer, as my earliest poet. But I would like to step back a generation to Sir Thomas Wyatt, who died nine years after the Queen was born. A trusted courtier of Henry VIII, he touches his lute as a troubadour. It is customary to compare the art of Sir Thomas Wyatt to that of the Latin poet, Horace. But Horace was a master of fine mosaic or a chiseler of marble. The courtier-poet must be musician rather than engraver; he was called upon to compose the music as well as the words of his poems. Every gentleman at the Court of Henry VIII, was, like the king himself, musician and poet. Music and poetry were not yet disassociated.

My lute awake! perform the last
Labour that thou and I shall waste,
And end that I have now begun;
And when this song is sung and past,
My lute be still, for I have done.

The praise of love, as a convention, was no longer tenable. It had come to England with Eleanor of Aquitaine, the mother of Richard Lion-Heart.

O Richard, O mon roi,
L'univers t'abandonne,

was sung outside the prison-tower, where the Saracens held the prince captive. But the prison-tower was nearer home now. I wonder, when Ben Jonson wrote the *Masque of Queens,* if he was influenced by those state processions, the Play of the people of the town of London. They had no other Play, then.

Samuel Daniel with his brother John, the musician, produced Masques which at one time threatened the popularity even of Ben Jonson. There were also the Masques of the Inner Temple, to which William Browne gave, for a time, new life. But the Masque was, like the conventional Shepherd and Shepherdess pastorals of Edmund Spenser and of his predecessor, Nicholas Breton, growing set and stylized. The Court was threatened by an outside factor. There was the new Globe Theatre to be considered. Certain plays could be cut to fit both Court and theatre, or extraneous dialogue could be added to a more or less complete comedy or tragedy. There was more than one set of conventions to be considered now. The bargeman and the beggar who loitered on the water-steps, had other spectacles beside the Royal Processions from Greenwich Palace to London. The Tower had had its fill of tragedy. Now tragedy found a place upon the boards, new planed, of the Globe Theatre.

Fear no more the heat o' the sun,
  Nor the furious winter's rages;
Thou thy worldly task hast done,
  Home art gone and ta'en thy wages:
Golden lads and girls all must,
As chimney-sweepers come to dust.

Home art gone—there was the mulberry-tree. Taffeta and damask had never held such colour. He had heard of a white mulberry that had turned purple, at the blood spilled of Grecian lovers. It had been necessary, he remembered, to enliven the history with mummery for the pit. But the gallants had not sat, dour-faced at this intrusion of the grotesque, into what happened to be originally intended as a tribute to *Cynthia. Cynthia* now, could be tricked up with a lantern, and *Wall* was a good part. Bottom the Weaver, as well as the hectoring row of courtiers, could criticise and condemn a *Midsummer Night's Dream.* There had been some awkwardness but the uncouth lad who scraped up the rushes had been induced to substitute for the decorous but unconvincing Thisbe of the first set of players. They were on and off the stage now. There was no *Wall* between.

> Fear no more the frown o' the great;
>   Thou art past the tyrant's stroke;
> Care no more to clothe and eat;
>   To thee the reed is as the oak;
> The sceptre, learning, physic, must
> All follow this and come to dust.

Still, there was hunger for fine damask, for purple hangings, for the anodine of incense, for the assurance of beatitude and the lost Host. The love of beauty had been satisfied by the dim, flower-stained light that fell, whether on a black velvet cloak or upon the sackcloth of a row of penitents. From the stench of life in the narrow, fulsome alleys, there was then, escape. It might be a cathedral unbarred, or a sacristy at the bridge-head. Even if death were waiting, for a moment, there was security. The Saints could be cajoled or bribed, or even tempted by promise of new altar cloth or a cup of silver. Death was a known entity, not only the skeleton on ropes that the older courtiers remembered in the *Miracles* of the Coventry *Corpus Christi,* or of Westminster, nearer home. He himself was not infallible.

The mind may compromise but the heart can not. Brilliant casuistry and subtle diplomacy in the end, made that compromise. But the English heart was not satisfied. The jewelled plate, the flower-stained windows had been marred by agents other than the assessors of the Crown. Priceless gems, it is true, can not intimidate the Spirit of God, but they can heal and console the Spirit of Man. The beauty displayed was, as it were, the dowry, brought by the Church, in the ceremony of betrothal. The Wedding took place at all hours of the day and night. This pledge was assurance of re-union after death. As God's Anointed, the King stood second only, in the hearts of loyal Englishmen. When the king broke faith, it was as if God had left them.

The mind might compromise, it was forced to do so. The heart could not.

But compromise was necessary.

We hear much of the sign-boards, set up in the Globe Theatre, this is a palace, this is the throne-room, this is the ante-chamber of His Excellency. We are apt to forget that many of the original masques and plays were acted in the palace itself, in the throne-room or in the ante-chamber. The decor, the decorations, the ornate imported mirrors, the purple hangings, the dais steps, the embroidered tapestry were all there. Why is this forgotten? The plays of Shakespeare had scenery waiting for them. Portia's caskets are produced by the Lord Treasurer, perhaps they are alms boxes from some magnificent cathedral. For the Capulet banquet, the scene is already laid. The musicians have only to tune up, in the gallery. Sumptuous plate and linen, looted from the Cardinal's palace, was shared alike by Montague and Capulet. Juliet's tomb was, no doubt, magnificently draped in violet. The candle-sticks recalled another canopy, another burial. The church was plundered by the palace; the palace became the background for new ritual. Although we hear so much of the mean equipment of the Globe Theatre, it must be remembered that, in the eyes of the producer at least, the place was overlaid with the memory of secret plunder. Death could yet be cajoled and men made happier.

We reach here, the high-water mark of human achievement. The Deity is seldom mentioned by William Shakespeare. It has been noted that in the famous speech of Henry V before Agincourt, he calls upon Saint Crispin and noticeably, except through the similarity of assonance, avoids direct appeal to the World's Saviour. Malvolio in *Twelfth Night,* who some think is a parody of Francis Bacon, others, a dissenting Puritan, addresses his champion as Jove. Princes of the church, before and after battle, discourse learnedly, it is true, on the rhetoric of religion. But these tirades or exhortations are in character, in costume, you might say. The dramatist himself remains discreetly non-committal. He is as abstract as Aeschylus, yet he speaks personally. He is diplomatic, yet he leaves us in no doubt as to how the scales of Justice will tilt. Sophocles' hero re-emerges as the Prince of Denmark. Aristotle's old truism, *katharsis* or cleansing, as the purport of all high tragedy, is obvious, yet the cleansing does not focus solely on the soul. The mighty penance of beholding in another's fate, the possible disaster, attendant on one's own headstrong pride, is conceded. We must find out for ourselves, what makes our neighbour's fault outrageous to us, and how our perversity hides from us our own sin. But sin is a word that is almost absent from the vast wealth of word and phrase found in the idiom of William Shakespeare.

Fear no more the lightning-flash,
  Nor the all-dreaded thunder-stone;
Fear not slander, censure rash;
  Thou hast finished joy and moan;

All lovers young, all lovers must
Consign to thee and come to dust.

All lovers young—lovers are always young. There is no sadness in this song. We know from the beginning, that the child, Fidele is not dead, but will re-emerge as the woman Imogen. To the devout Catholic, this assurance would not be necessary. To the devout Christian, unwilling to renounce the hope, implicit in his religion, there was now only subterfuge or disillusion. Into the great vacuum, left by the flame that had hung alike over Catholic and Protestant martyr, there rushed with the whirlwind of the Pentecost, this host, drunk with new wine. It was the wine of the Spirit, certainly. Formerly, those condemned to life, equally with those condemned to death, knew the way out of and into darkness. If there was doubt or indecision, it could be countered by the logic of the church. There was no logic, no reason now. There was no safety. Mary had sought to avenge the martyrs of her mother's faith. Elizabeth again, had re-animated her father's frenzy against the monasteries and hospitals, re-established by her sister, Mary. Who would come next?

This was the question in the minds of Webster, Middleton, Dekker, Ford, Massinger and that host who stood in the black shadow of the charred city. They answered it. It has been noted that many of these extravagant tragedies had a renaissance or Italian setting. Rome is never the scene of these many plays. When Shakespeare addresses Rome, it is the Rome of political faction, antedating the long drawn out religious faction. But Venice, Milan, Verona, Sicily, Naples are annexed. *Let Rome in Tiber melt* was spoken by Marc Antony, but the poet was possibly thinking of the ruin wrought in his own country, by other Caesars and other Antonys and by the lure of other Cleopatras. This historical play comes late. His English kings have had their say, during the life-time of the great Queen. Now Shakespeare goes back into time, to Egypt and to Ancient Britain.

But Egypt and Ancient Britain, legendary or historical, have boundaries. The English kings who preceded them in the sequence of historical plays, stood equally, for all their roses white and red, upon solid ground. There had been no poets since Chaucer. He might have appeared in a scene from *Henry V* or *Henry VI*. He seems as legendary as a character in a play. We have *Richard III,* and there is no poet in it, nor incidental song and minstrelsy. The reign of Henry VII produced John Skelton, standing alone, an English poet with a scattering of unimportant, imported French about him. Henry VIII himself a musician, encouraged song and poetry, but it was indigenous to the Court. There is Thomas, Lord Vaux, as well as Henry Howard, Earl of Surrey and Sir Thomas Wyatt. From the universities, we have Nicholas Grimald and John Heywood, the Oxford dramatist who became Court jester. But theirs was the stylized, exquisite music that was first introduced by the Provence troubadours, imported as we have said, by England's fifth queen, the mother of Richard I. It had taken four hundred years for the Provençal lyrist to establish his identity, but Eleanor's *School of Love* found strange pupils at the Court of Henry VIII.

Now cease, my lute! this is the last
Labour that thou and I shall waste,
And ended is that we begun;
Now is this song both sung and past—
My lute be still, for I have done.

For a short space, the lute was still indeed. Edward VI and Mary had no plays, written for them or about them. For ten years there is a gap in time. Edward VI, a ward under the protection (or its opposite) of various Court officials, might almost have been that other Edward who with his brother Richard was deposed and done away with in the Tower. The shadow of the Tower grows blacker, though we thought we had moved out of its compass, with the death of Henry VIII. But the death of Edward VI is still a mystery, unlike that of his predecessor Edward V, and his brother Richard. Mary Tudor is the first queen of England, in her own right. How far the atrocities committed in her name were actually of her connivance or due to the power of Rome, will also remain a mystery. Now, terror took the place of sanctuary. The Cathedral door was still unbarred, but its crypt held prisoners, swept into that dark vault, with no knowledge that they were suspect, as they knelt at the altar-rail, either wrapt in contemplation or for purposes of policy.

For ten years the fate of England and the world hung in the balance. William of Normandy was affiliated with the Latins. The Court and wealthy land-owners followed the custom and religion of the conqueror. But beneath the solid tyranny of the first king of England, there was that native culture of Caedmon and Cynewulf, the Christian Saxon poets. Their names recall *King Lear* and again, *Cymbeline*. They ante-dated Normandy by some five hundred years. They again had succeeded the first Latins by roughly five hundred years. Behind William, there was one thousand years of animosity. Though the first William was affiliated with Rome, it was not the Rome of the conqueror Caesar.

It was as if the ten years of Edward VI and Mary had broken the crust, hardened by time, of a not yet extinct volcano.

Beneath the lava and ashes of Norman conquest, a living world lay buried. It had seeped up from time to time, since the days of William. It had drawn the best of his warriors away from England. The Holy Wars were an excuse for travel, more than an excuse, a necessity. That lure of foreign places, was really love of home, their own native boundaries. The urge would be satisfied for a time by wars in England. When a sort of transitional peace fell upon the prince and barons, it was time to leave. So Richard Lion-Heart with his train of princely ruffians leaves England. Later the same predominant instinct seizes a restless people. Incited again by an Italian precedent, Drake and Raleigh follow the example of the Venetians, John and Sebastian Cabot, and the great Magellan.

The volcano was seething. Flame and fire had undermined the Pope's authority. If that could be defied, and now (in the reign of Elizabeth), with impunity, then anything could happen. The process was partly unconscious but rebellion was at work here, and the carefully wrought, balanced sequence of dramatic action, on and off the stage, became independent of authority.

It is one thing to cast off authority, it is another thing to cast off love. As authority waned, love grew. Rome was like a great bee-hive, but we are apt to forget that at the time of Caedmon, Rome was only one of several centres of equal power and authority. Augustine came to England from Africa, and the Church of Africa, at that time, stood equal with the Church of Rome. Simon de Montford, the William of his day, had made his final inroads against the Church of Provence. The Inquisition had destroyed the cult of Our Lady, as an embodiment or rather personification of the Church Spiritual, but the Lady banished from the churches of Provence, found refuge elsewhere. The troubadours, wandering along the flowering highways, carried with them the lute that Thomas Wyatt, some three hundred years later, touched for the last time, at the Court of Henry VIII. For Eleanor, remembering her own girlhood and the fleeting smile of a lost lover in Provence, had tempered her exile in the bitter north, by endeavouring to introduce into the brutish throng of that alien baron, Henry II, some shadow of the memory of games, played in earnest and vows spoken in the phrase and rhythm of the early church. The *School of Love* was related to another and now also dispersed religion, the cult of the original kings of Britain and of Brittany. The Round Table, as is now recognised, is a symbol of the last Supper. Eleanor herself was, no doubt, unaware of this, but the reign of the Plantagenets was marked by a later flowering of the "lost" religion. It was not only the genista or the golden gorse, that burst into a flame of blossom, it was the *courtezia* of love, as well as the *aubade* of the musicians and poets of Provence. That influence became a sort of courtly convention; it is implicit in the plays, *John* and *Richard II,* which deal with the third and with the last of the eight Plantagenet kings. With the sensitive, wavering Richard II, the golden flower is trodden underfoot, in the hundred years' frightful conflict over roses, white and red.

These are Shakespeare's kings. They may be England's, but that sometimes seems irrelevant and unimportant. Without these plays and the later comedies and tragedies, England, in the light of the world's culture, would rank at best, as a sort of bulwark of material strength, *this fortress built by Nature for herself.* It is the weakness, not the strength of England that defies time. It is the death in poverty, of Edmund Spenser, returned, a failure, from Ireland; it is the recklessness of Sir Philip Sidney, whose *your need is greater than mine* has become proverbial; it is Sir Walter Raleigh who with his last breath, gives the lie to pomp and circumstance; Kit Marlowe with *if all the pens that ever poets held;* Thomas Nash, a voluntary witness that *the plague full swift goes by;* Ben Jonson with his sublimization of the black-draped barges at the foot of the Tower stairs, in his *Masque of Queens,* and of John Donne's

> One short sleep past, we wake eternally,
> And Death shall be no more; Death, thou shalt die;

it is Sir Henry Wotton with his hopeless devotion to Elizabeth of Bohemia, and Essex in the Tower, fighting and defiant, like Raleigh, to the end.

Simon de Montford had sworn to exterminate the last, living member of the Church of Provence. He succeeded in driving the worship of Love into the high-ways and by-ways of Europe. But Rome itself was not immunized. It was the Kathars of Provence who first inaugurated the system of wandering mendicants. Although the out-cast laid aside his sandals and robe, his transformation was but superficial. As he wandered, a troubadour, from castle-fortress to castle-fortress, he was (unknown to the lords of Aquitaine and Provence), spreading the germs of deadly heresy, the worship of beauty. This worship, forced to renounce the official language of the Church, disguised itself in terms of earthly passion. But this passion was never requited. In other words, the love of the troubadour was love of the Spiritual. This love could not be satisfied on earth. Later, it became formalized into the code, set forth in the *Morte d'Arthur.* The knight wore his lady's favour, but it was understood that that lady was set apart, a convention or ideal to which he was dedicated. So subtle was the influence of the mendicant, cast out of the Church of Provence, that a further transformation, or a turn in the road, brings him to Assisi. Francis was brought up, as all the young noblemen of his time, on tales of knightly valour and the poems of these same troubadours. Renouncing wealth and privilege, he takes to himself the rough garment of sack-cloth. Francis brings back the cult of Our Lady Poverty to Rome.

Later, the Saint of Avila, also brought up on tales of knightly valour, leaves her dowry and her palace, and in the end, gathered her novices about her and lays the foundation of the new order of Carmelites, as Francis had done of the Franciscans. It will be noted that Francis overcame insuperable difficulties before his cult of Our Lady Poverty proved acceptable to the Holy Father at Rome, and that Teresa was actually, during the writing of her great book, under the suspicion and, at one time, the interdict of the Inquisition.

The poet is always suspect. In spite of himself and all his good intentions, he comes to no good. We have seen how the germs of this deadly heresy flourished in England. These heretics were the more the martyrs, in that they themselves were unconscious of the source of their inspiration. Reason, as I have said, was well within the intellectual range of each one of them. But love was stronger. The power of love built up a kingdom. When his trust in Church and Court fell, in the bitter dissensions begun by Henry VIII, the suspect instinctively began to prepare for himself his recompense. It was the children of the martyrs who fulfilled the unconscious longing of the older generation.

Two roads were open to these heretics or poets. There was the way of stark reality and there was escape from that reality. There was one door always open, but they looked fearful and diminished, straight through the portals of Death, and saw what was or was not there. It was no longer possible to accept dogma or even inspiration from another, as to the steps down to Hell or those leading up to Heaven. They must see for themselves and they did see. As the boundaries of the known world, so the boundaries of the unknown were extended. This was a spiritual necessity.

Wit with his wantonness
Tasteth death's bitterness,

but the bitterness was not the idea of absolute extinction. The lesser and the greater poet alike met in the unanimous acceptance of one article of faith.

> For in that sleep of death what dreams may come
> When we have shuffled off this mortal coil,
> Must give us pause.

The dream was greater than reality. Out of it, they built a city, comparable to Augustine's *City of God,* or a fortress as formidable as the *Castle* of Teresa. Francis himself might have learned much from the blossoms of Robert Herrick or the *lilies of all kinds* of that *Winter's Tale.* The spiritual inheritance, substantially absorbed by Rome, was not lost. It had been carried, not in iron chests guarded by the vanguard of a conquering army, but it had blown on the wind, as the jongleur, the jester, the beggar wandered, himself suspect, from court to court. He gathered sometimes as he went, strange flowers, it is true, but the seeds of the faith, in the end, blown by the tempest or carried in the dowry-chest of the girl from the south, took root.

An exotic flower—it blossomed only in the queen's tiring-room or later, in the king's banquet-hall. Then it was hewn down. But the roots of that flower still flourished and sent out thorny branches. In France, the popularity of the *Roman de la Rose* was at its height, when Richmond proclaims, at the end of *Richard III,*

> We will unite the white rose and the red.

Theoretically, the Tudors bore the red and the white rose, in the heraldic wreath around the lions and lilies. But Henry VIII proved the fallacy of this presumption, for Mary re-animated the old dissension, and to Elizabeth, all roses were one colour.

If we presume symbolically, that the white rose is a symbol of spiritual love, it is obvious that the red rose is not only a symbol, but an actual image of the heart. The blood-red blossom is also symbol of the martyr's death. The white rose, drained of its life-blood, is not a symbol only, but a phantom as well, and a phantom more real than the incontinent world of cathedral and of court. *Death thou shalt die* was spoken by one of the arch-heretics, whether officially a Catholic or of the disinherited Church of England makes no difference. There were no boundaries, and though actually each might walk in hourly fear of the opposing faction, there was, in the innermost circle of the heretical church, no schism and no dissension.

Official death was more likely to track down the fortunate. Marlowe was early recognized as a dramatist and he was as well, as has recently been established, a secret agent of no mean ability. I have said that he acted himself to death and that the same is true of Raleigh. Spenser was selected or favoured by the Lord-Lieutenant of Ireland for diplomatic reasons; Ben Jonson, having had his childhood blighted by poverty, devoted himself to producing those processions of animated abstractions. These four outstanding heretics were marked down, from the first, for disaster. Though Ben Jonson's disaster was perhaps unrecognized, it is none the less obvious. His success was attained at the price of renouncing genius for talent.

Thomas Nash, we may imagine, was not so much a victim of circumstance, as of voluntary dedication, *The plague full swift goes by,* and Webster, a child or youth, sees death in its most abhorrent aspect of gradual or partial decay. To the observer, whether physician like Thomas Lodge or grave-digger like John Donne, there can be no possible compromise. The dedicated may rush to the altar-rail for absolution, or he may seek out a place in the Inn.

He may have, indeed he must inevitably have passed through the same charnel-house which Juliet in her ravings, reproduces for us and the traditional grave-digger in *Hamlet* offers us, in the death-head of poor Yorick. *Alas, poor Yorick*—the memory of this earthy skull served at the end as a reminder to this cautious citizen of Stratford to be careful of his last belongings: *Good Frend, for Iesus sake forbeare.*

He was sitting with Michael Drayton and Ben Jonson after dinner, one spring evening. These were old friends. Drayton was one year older. Was he perhaps a cousin or friend of one of the younger Lucys? He is known to have been connected with the neighbouring Warwickshire nobility. The lad may have secretly hunted with Michael Drayton and some of the younger Lucys. The older Lucys would have kept to themselves, their own rule and convention would have excluded the son of John Shakespeare and Mary Arden from their hunting-parties.

Ben Jonson is still younger. There is eight years difference in their ages. Ben Jonson in his avid pursuit of learning—of books—had condescended to take part in one of his own, not too successful productions. He paid the young man what he could but regretted, from the first, that he could teach him nothing. Ben Jonson's brilliant mind, however, had been recognized. He himself and Fletcher had had many set-backs. It seemed nothing could intimidate Ben Jonson. He sat there, solid yet easily swayed by the passing whims of Court and fashion. He did not ask Jonson the news, this time. Drayton went on talking.

Long-purples grew beside the Avon. Some called the flowering spray of willow-herb, long-purples. But that was not what he meant when he hesitated, trying to remember what Mary had first called the others. They were not harebells. He held the stems toward her. She never called them deadmen's-fingers, he knew that. He couldn't remember what she had called them. He saw the fire reflected in the row of pewter plates. Then he was back in the kitchen and smelt wood-smoke and spice, and the delicate fragrance of the flowers with the too-long green-white stems that he held toward Mary Arden. There were mistakes like that. And the rhymes had sometimes caused dissension in the green-room. Not like Marlowe, they said. No, he wasn't like Marlowe, nor was he much like the others. Fletcher was more tolerant—but take Ben there. Michael hardly counted. Michael remembered exploits, when moonlight on the snow bewitched his arrows. Michael had admired him for his archery, and that early infatuation had spoiled his later judgments. But taken all in all, he hadn't done so badly. There was the new house and the garden.

The wind was blowing from the Cotswolds. Lear had wandered among those scattered boulders, and from a hillock, he had watched till *Birnam wood be come to Dunsinane.* When it did come, he heard a shout, *Hail king! for so thou art.* The old king was raving and blind, but that was earlier. Or was it later? Malcolm did not have the last word, however. Perhaps he should have cut the act, after Macbeth's *to-morrow and to-morrow and to-morrow.* The rest of the scene was unnecessary, but there was always that space between the end and the departure of the players. That had to be filled in. Each actor wanted to return and make his presence felt, after the play was actually over. But Prospero had had the last word. Yes, that was a tempest. He remembered how he had lost his way, stumbling over the stony ground. The casement rattled and the fire sent out a cloud of smoke, as a late guest brushed past them. He opened the door and the cold wind rushed in; Michael was still talking.

It was an old controversy. Was or was not the Grecian right in the assumption that certain unities were necessary? Unity of time, space and so on. But he had long since despaired of these same unities. It was hardly a matter of unities, it was holding the audience that concerned him. As to time and place—there was *Tamburlaine*. There was no break there. *Tamburlaine the Great* needed no Touchstone nor any Twelfth Night fool, with *Come away, come away, Death* to distract an audience. Whether or not that play needed to be enlivened by unities broken and shattered, was really beyond his knowing. But Ben knew the answer to these things. There was Aristotle and the final word, *katharsis*—that was Greek certainly.

> And sighed his soul toward the Grecian tents
> Where Cressid lay that night.

The *Merchant* lacked unity, there was no doubt about that. It was Marlowe's *Jew* that had given him the idea, but the Jew of Venice did not succeed as the *Jew of Malta* had done. Ben Jonson was right there.

Juliet was still worse. It was two plays really. One play was over when Mercutio cried,

> They have made worms' meat of me.

It had started as a romance, but as the Jew spoiled the unity of the *Merchant*, so some alien voice had shouted down the lovers' triumph. He had tried to intimidate them, or rather Mercutio had, by delaying the action (or trying to delay Romeo), by a long poem that should have been left out, or at best or worst, gone into the *Dream*. It was Drayton's idea really—Oberon and *Midsummer Night's Dream*. There was no room for deadmen's-fingers or long-purples there.

We know there was *courtezia.* There was as well, the *aubade* which Juliet tried in vain to nullify. Love fulfilled was powerless against the old forces of unconscious longing for ultimate union. All worldly gifts must be offered—the gift of wealth and leisure, in the case of Francis, the gift of convention and the world's commendation, in the case of Teresa. The soul, blindly seeking, had found haven or sanctuary in the Office of the Mass, and the mind, tortured and disintegrating, was lulled by the anodine of countless *Aves* and *Pater Nosters.* Even when the body was ill-clothed, there were the wonders of the dowry of the Saints to be gaped at, and the candle-sticks and costly vestments of the servers. The world was clothed in satin and rich velvet; one might even brush against a sable or an ermine border. One beheld an assembly in this drawing-room that one would never, under any circumstances, be permitted to mingle with, elsewhere. There were now open cathedral doors, but with all the effort to re-establish the Latin ritual in its English trappings, there was something lacking. It was not for nothing that Simon de Montford had plundered the Holy Land of Provence. Not all the rhythm and metre was the property of the wandering mendicant, or at least, it did not remain so. Into the pagan litanies of Rome, there crept a tender, wistful note. The *Fioretti* vied with the porphyry and marble of Diocletian, and the Child, with the discarded myths of Capitoline Jupiter.

The Child was the symbol of ultimate union.

Juliet was a child, really. Controversy as to the marriageable age of girls in Renaissance Italy does not alter that. In fact, Juliet was two children, though one of them was doomed. Both of them were doomed, finally, for how could one of them live without the other?

Parental authority had killed Juliet. She died that morning when he left her. Friar Lawrence, gathering his herbs, was Francis come to life, in his sandals and brown habit. He could delay the final dissolution by a few days, no longer. The Church, the Bride of Provence (or Verona) lay decked in her renaissance marriage garments and crowned with flowers. She is lying in her bride-bed, and parents and household pass before her; they genuflect or kneel, till finally Friar Lawrence himself takes over responsibility.

He will steal this Bride of Provence from her father's very palace.

Montague and Capulet (the eternal faction) have both been forced to relinquish the claim to spiritual inheritance. There will be a new life, another renaissance, when the bridegroom returns from Mantua. We have only to wait. Friar Lawrence, Francis and the gentle Shakespeare wait with us. But events beyond their control, take over the play and the lovers are united, as only they could be, beyond the grave. Romeo returns too soon or too late. Juliet wakes too soon or too late.

The fire is going out. Ben Jonson and Michael Drayton are still arguing. There was that *katharsis*. The body of society, the body of life could not be healed. There was only one solution, but though he had intended to follow the plot as Fletcher had outlined it for him from the Italian folio, the story had misled him. He had, however, taken the main events. But unlike Marlowe's *Tamburlaine,* this lesser tragedy had been interrupted. It was not only that Mercutio became too important in the first part, and so cut the play in half. The play faltered in any case. Juliet's nurse intruded. The parents were bodiless, abstractions like Ben Jonson's. Paris, the worldly suitor, was unconvincing. He did not really love her. He would never have died at her tomb, fighting the legitimate bridegroom.

All lovers young, all lovers must
Consign to thee and come to dust.

All lovers young—lovers are always young. But the child Fidele, in *Cymbeline,* is not two children but one—so later, William Shakespeare. Imogen is Fidele, just as Rosalind is Ganymede. Juliet is herself only, but she seeks for ultimate fulfilment in another. But according to the old creed and canon of the Kathars, that was not possible. Now we have come back to Eleanor of Aquitaine and the *School of Love.*

What he taught, he taught unconsciously. The ache and urge for the ideal had been thwarted. No doubt, what was lost by Mary was gained by Elizabeth. But still, through Elizabethan poetry, there is this obsession with the lost Virgin. The moon, a symbol of chastity, was associated with the Mother of God. Now Cynthia herself must be invoked, in the guise of Queen Elizabeth. But there were younger adepts. To them, no doubt, there was another schism. We hear nothing of this, but the playwright shows his rebellion in the unevenness of the Venetian story, and even more so

In fair Verona, where we lay our scene.

They were children, huddled together in Judith's bed. Capulet found only one of them. The nurse was wailing, in her tiresome fashion. Friar Lawrence explained it afterwards, but it was too late. The unities of time and place had been disregarded. Michael had a theory, it was, as was usual with him, compound of moon-beams and of cobwebs. He had always re-written his stanzas and re-worked them. Now he was returning to his old *Nymphidia.* There, he had assembled his elves and fairies, his ant, his bee, his

Hobgoblin in the manner of an old wives' tale. Now he remembered *Agincourt* and how, after the fall of the curtain, his own audience had forgotten him and called for Michael Drayton. It was like that. But *Henry V* was a success all told. It may have been Michael's ballad that had made it so. He watched Juliet sleeping.

Would she ever wake up and if she did, who would tell her about Hamnet? *But that the dread of something after death*—that was later, but it was Juliet's fear. The lines were overlaid with the horror of the old plague. But she would wake up. Or perhaps she would not wake up. Or she would wake and find Hamnet dead, and refuse to live without him. Michael said it was Queen Eleanor who brought the song to England. A French queen. But Michael said she was Richard's mother. Which Richard? Not Richmond's rival? No, there were three before Richard III, if you count the child. There was the other Edward but that was all long after. How had he gone? But that was Mary's brother. Mary? He smelt the saffron cakes, as she drew them from the oven. He held the flowers toward her. He had forgotten what she called them—not deadmen's-fingers, anyway.

He thought they were talking about Aristotle and the *katharsis,* the healing implicit in those unities. But it was Queen Eleanor and Provence and a ritual that had to do with Mary. No, it wasn't Mary. It was, it seemed, the Church Spiritual. It was the Bride of God these Kathars, as Michael called them, worshipped. But wasn't every church that? He couldn't follow any further. They were all heretics. Was he recalling the old days of the boy Edward and his sister, Mary?

But it was not Agincourt now that roused him. It was the thought of the island before Henry. But that was another Henry, the third, Michael was insisting. He hadn't really interrupted. The fire had gone out, and the wind from the door cut through his shoulder-blades. He shifted his chair, a hint they should be going. It was the worship of beauty, Michael was concluding, that William and the barons had clamped down. But hadn't the French brought in beauty? Michael was patient with him. France was not all Normandy, Michael was saying to him.

Of course, he knew that.

Cynthia had not satisfied him. Moonlight on the snow had spoiled him for any other. He was glad to get back to Stratford.

Never harm,
Nor spell nor charm
Come our lovely lady nigh.

She spoke of grapes, the vine, remembering Antony and the purple sails. But that was not Imogen, it went back further. Her claim on Caesar had been disregarded. Antony by her jealousy had been goaded to death. Then she died. But she died splendidly, although she feared the mockery of the players, after the victory of the new Triumvirs. Actium. Now he was back with the old dilemma. Suppose she woke up and found him, or suppose she woke up and didn't find him. *What's this? A cup, closed in my true love's hand?* Would it have been better, after all, to have had her die first? Michael went on talking.

Antony had died first. But that was another cup. Antony was so much younger. But that happened three years before her death and then, Cleopatra was much older. There was really no comparison. Poor Essex. Raleigh had succeeded him, but under another tyrant. His *Virginia* was enough of a compliment to last a life-time—her life-time. That was Michael's too. *The Virginian Voyage.* He would have been off with them, but he had discovered his own island. England?

We are such stuff as dreams are made on and if actively, we are restricted, we escape. It was so, from the beginning. Their Warwickshire vines were too low-growing, they said, but the small berries were sweet. He held the goblet to the light but the tapers reflected too many pictures in the glass. The flagon was empty.

Francis Bacon talked endlessly. Mantua, Padua, Vienna, Sicily, Ravenna, Venice, Verona—he stared at him. The face, lean and brown, the thin fingers, the hollow at his temples—his hands again. Italy! *Let Rome in Tiber melt,* but it wasn't Rome he thought of. The Venetian goblet was filled with white wine. He did not touch it. He watched the hand that moved so eloquently, and the shadow of the hand. He noted the cuff, pleated with a thread of dark-wine silk, and a knot of the same colour at the wrist. His beard was trimmed to an even finer point than usual. He spoke in firm, fine measure. He spoke as he looked, a courtier and a gentleman. What he said had an assurance that was English, the English of the schoolmen. It was not the language of the ordinary courtier. Most of them had gone. Francis Bacon had delayed him. He was a man of about his own age, yet he seemed infinitely older. He had had the advantage of Trinity and Cambridge. There was something he and Raleigh had in common. He knew what it was. Deliberately, he turned the long-stemmed chalice in his own somewhat shorter, stronger fingers. The glass stem would snap, if he were not careful. The glass was gold and the wine was gold, yet neither quite matched the yellow flame of candles. The words of Francis Bacon were deliberate, diplomatic. He understood them. He was quite prepared to under-score the dialogue, so that as usual, the players came within the range of Cynthia's shining. He did not have to be told to do that, nor was even a diplomatic hint necessary. He kept his archer's gaze on the fine, dark features. He must not look at the chalice nor the gold wine. Mantua, Padua—he steadied his arm. He tightened the bow-string. But he would wait.

The vine-stem did not snap—he meant the wine-stem. He meant the stalk of the wine glass. But he was looking at another. He had managed with Hippolyta, the Amazon, the Virgin Huntress—all that mixed up with Michael's Titania and Oberon. These things were not difficult. But he was looking at Ben now. It was not that he regretted his refusal of the offer. His French was adequate. Francis Bacon had stipulated nothing. Another gentleman was needed. The glass stem had not broken. There was John Shakespeare's concession, of course—a Swan and an Arrow with suitable Latin, was a protection. But it was no protection—why did he remember now? Michael had more than made up for the Lucy insult.

Still he looked at Francis Bacon, and though he saw arcades and the sun falling on a shallow lagoon through the arch of a bridge, and a marble column frightened him with an ecstasy, too great to be borne—though they were not there, he felt them, *things in heaven and earth*—and knew that the flowers would be different and the flowers would be the same, like the tiny pansy border in the illuminated book that Michael showed him, from his father's library—though he felt, rather than heard their voices and the resonance of them echoing, as they could never do in England, his glance did not waver. No, he thanked Francis Bacon for his offer.

He had died first, the cup of death clasped in his hand. There was still a stain of purple in the wine glass, he himself held. They had stopped talking. He remembered that other golden wine and the chalice, like the cup of a day-lily. The day came too swiftly, for the day brought darkness, the darkness of knowledge. They were huddled together in Judith's bed, as he remembered them last together, though that was after he left London. That is, he remembered, as he drove his tired horse through Oxford, on the way back. He remembered them huddled together. They were cold. Did he speak harshly to Hamnet? He could not remember. He remembered words out of his own play,

> Or bid me go into a new-made grave
> And hide me with a dead man in his shroud.

That was the child, Juliet, Judith. He himself had prophesied the whole thing. If he had not written the play, it never would have happened.

Now he saw why he had not gone with Francis Bacon, as one of the minor courtiers, on the Queen's business. The Queen's business was waiting beyond Oxford. He hardly understood the implication or the impact of what he felt. It was a thing sensed, not thought. But there were words for it. Michael had just said something that had stirred a memory. It was Judith, it was Juliet, it was Queen Eleanor. It was a plum-coloured sleeve and the shadow of a thin hand and the feel of the glass stem between his thumb and finger. It was the sense of the moment when the slender stem would snap—and waiting. It was keeping back something. They had all, always kept back something. The metres ran on, recklessly or bound or ruled rather, like Campion's music. But something snapped. It was not the Venetian glass stem. He had come home because he loved Judith.

September 19
November 1
1946

The following dates of birth and death have been used in the structure of *The Guest*.

Bacon, Francis	1561—1626
Beaumont, Francis	1584—1616
Beaumont, John	1583—1627
Breton, Nicholas	1545?–1626?
Browne, William	1591—1643
Campion, Thomas	1567—1620
Carew, Thomas	1598?–1639?
Chapman, George	1559?–1634
Constable, Henry	1562—1613
Crashaw, Richard	1613?–1649
Daniel, John	? —1625
Daniel, Samuel	1562—1619
Davenant, William	1606—1668
Davison, Francis	1575?–1619?
Dekker, Thomas	1570?–1641?
Devereux, Robert	1567—1601
Donne, John	1572—1631
Drayton, Michael	1563—1631
Drummond, William	1585—1649
Dyer, Edward	c.1540—1607
Fletcher, Giles	c.1588—1623
Fletcher, John	1579—1625
Fletcher, Phineas	1582—1650
Ford, John	1586—1640?
Greene, Robert	1560?–1592
Greville, Fulke	1554—1628
Grimald, Nicholas	1519—1562

Herbert, Edward	1583—1648
Herbert, George	1593—1633
Herrick, Robert	1591—1674
Heywood, John	c.1497–c.1580
Heywood, Thomas	1575?–c.1650
Howard, Henry	1517?–1547
Jonson, Ben	1572—1637
King, Henry	1592—1669
Lodge, Thomas	1558?–1625
Lovelace, Richard	1618—1658
Lyly, John	1554?–1606
Marlowe, Christopher	1564—1593
Massinger, Philip	1583—1640
Middleton, Thomas	1570?–1627
Nash, Thomas	1567—1601
Peele, George	1558—1597?
Quarles, Francis	1592—1644
Raleigh, Walter	1552—1618
Rowlands, Richard	1565—1620
Rowley, William	1585?–1642?
Shakespeare, William	1564—1616
Shirley, James	1596—1666
Sidney, Philip	1554—1586
Southwell, Robert	1561—1595
Spenser, Edmund	1553?–1599
Strode, William	1599?–1645
Suckling, John	1609—1642
Vaux, Thomas	1510—1556
Waller, Edmund	1606—1687
Webster, John	1580?–1630
Wotton, Henry	1568—1639
Wyatt, Thomas	1503—1542